MacOS Fundamentals

Big Sur Edition

Kevin Wilson

www.elluminetpress.com

MacOS Fundamentals: Big Sur Edition

iStock.com/golibo, PeopleImages, ymgerman. Photo 130859010 © Kaspars Grinvalds - Dreamstime.com. Photo 103557713 © Konstantin Kolosov - Dreamstime.com. Yuri Arcurs via Getty Images

Publisher: Elluminet Press
Director: Kevin Wilson
Lead Editor: Steven Ashmore
Technical Reviewer: Mike Taylor, Robert Ashcroft
Copy Editors: Joanne Taylor, James Marsh
Proof Reader: Steven Ashmore
Indexer: James Marsh
Cover Designer: Kevin Wilson

eBook versions and licenses are also available for most titles. Any source code or other supplementary materials referenced by the author in this text is available to readers at
www.elluminetpress.com/resources

For detailed information about how to locate your book's resources, go to
www.elluminetpress.com/resources

Table of Contents

About the Author 11

Acknowledgements 13

MacOS Big Sur 14

What's New? 15
Available Macs 18
Macbook Air.. 18
Macbook Pro 18
iMac... 19
iMac Pro... 19
Mac Pro.. 19
Mac Mini... 19

Setting up Your Mac 20

Upgrading to Big Sur.. 21
Power Up 23
Power Down 24
Starting your Mac for the First Time........................... 25
Create a New ID 32
iCloud.. 33
iCloud Drive Setup... 34
iCloud Sync 35
Storage Management.. 36
Setup Internet... 37
WiFi 37
Using an Ethernet Cable 38
Phone Tethering... 41
Mobile USB Modems 42
Virtual Private Networks... 43
Using a VPN Service 43
Manual Setup 44
Connecting Peripherals 45
System Preferences 47
Add a Printer... 49
Connect Printer to WiFi 51
Other Email Accounts 52
Additional Users.. 55
Login Options.. 57
Change Passwords 59
Mac Password 59
Apple ID Password 60
Setup Apple Pay 61

Setup Apple Pay on a Macbook.. 63
Touch ID... 64
Dark Mode & Light Mode.. 66
Setup your Trackpad.. 67
Setup your Mouse 69
Screensavers... 70
Dynamic Desktop.. 71
Desktop Wallpaper 72
Managing Displays 73
System Audio... 76
Pairing Bluetooth Devices.. 78
Fonts 79
Find My 81
    Setup *81*
    Locating & Taking Action.. *82*
    Sharing Locations *83*
    Check Someone's Location *84*
Time Machine Backup.. 85
    Setting Up Backups *85*
    Restoring Items.. *89*
Transfer Files from a Windows PC 90
Transfer Files from an old Mac 93

Getting Around Your Mac.. **94**

The Desktop.. 95
The Menu Bar 96
    Application Menu *96*
    Status Menu *96*
The Dock 97
Stacks.. 99
Launchpad... 100
Spaces & Mission Control... 102
Finder... 104
    File View Style.. *105*
    Markup *108*
    Markup using your iPad *110*
    Tags... *112*
    Tagging Files *114*
    Smart Folders *115*
    Quick Preview Files *118*
    Compress Files *118*
    Accessing External Drives *119*
    Accessing Data CDs and DVDs... *120*
    Sharing Files on a Network *121*
    Connect to a Shared Folder on Another Computer *124*
    Finder Preferences.. *125*

iCloud Drive... 127
    Using iCloud Drive... *127*
    iCloud Drive File Sharing.. *129*
Managing App Windows 132
    Moving a Window *132*
    Resizing a Window... *133*
    Minimise, Maximise & Close a Window *134*
Spotlight Search.. 135
Notification Centre 136
    Notifications... *137*
        Banners *137*
        Alerts *137*
        Badges *137*
        Notification Settings *138*
    Widgets.. *139*
Control Centre 140
Handoff.. 142
SideCar.. 144
Universal Clipboard... 148
Using Siri... 149
Voice Control 150
Voice Dictation.. 151
Using Apple Pay on your Mac 153
Auto Unlock.. 154
The Mac Keyboard... 156
    The Command Key... *156*
    The Option Key.. *157*
    The Control Key... *157*
    The Function Key.. *157*
    Executing Keyboard Shortcuts *157*
Useful Keyboard Shortcuts.. 158
MacOS Startup Keys 159
Making Gestures... 160
    One Finger Point and Tap... *160*
    Right Click *160*
    Two Finger Scroll... *161*
    Two Finger Rotate *161*
    Two Finger Swipe... *162*
    Four Finger Open Launchpad.. *162*
Magic Mouse 163
    Left Click... *163*
    Right Click *163*
    Scrolling.. *164*
    Swipe.. *164*
Find your Mouse Pointer 165
The Touch Bar 166

Touch Bar Layout *166*
Control Strip *167*
Application Strip *167*
Customise Touch Bar *169*
Taking Screenshots 170
Screen Recording 171
Split Screen Mode 172
Digitally Sign a Document 174
Keychain 176

Using Applications **178**
Launching Your Applications 179
Killing Unresponsive Apps 181
App Store 182
App Tabs 184
Maps 185
Exploring Places *185*
Share a Location *186*
Share a Map *186*
Favourites *187*
Drop a Pin *187*
Guides *188*
Public Transport Routes *190*
Driving Directions *191*
Walking Directions *192*
Look Around *192*
Explore in 3D *193*
Look Inside *193*
Apple Books 194
Notes 198
Calendar 200
Adding an Event *200*
Create a Calendar *201*
Export Calendar *201*
Import Calendar *202*
Add an Event from Email *202*
Subscribing to Public Calendar *203*
Sharing Calendars & Creating Public Calendars ... *204*
Image Capture 205
Photobooth 206
DVDs & Blu-rays 208
Voice Memos 210
Recording Memos *211*
Renaming Memos *212*
Trim a Memo *213*
News 214

Terminal 216
    Opening Terminal 216
    Giving Commands 217
Pages App 218
    Getting Started 218
    Formatting Text 220
    Adding a Picture 221
    Instant Alpha 222
    Saving 223
    Sharing and Collaboration 224
Keynote App 225
    Getting Started 225
    Editing a Slide 226
    Adding a New Slide 227
    Adding Media 227
    Animations 228
    Slide Transitions 230
    Formatting Text Boxes 230
    Formatting Text Inside Textboxes 231
    Adding Styles to Textboxes 232
    Saving 234
Numbers App 235
    Getting Started 235
    Building a Spreadsheet 237
    Entering Data 237
    Changing Data Types 238
    Adding Formulas 238
    Adding Functions 239
    Saving 239

Internet, Email & Communications **240**

Using Safari to Browse the Web 241
    Launching Safari 241
    Customise your Homepage 242
    Using Safari 243
    Browsing Tabs 243
    Show all Browsing Tabs 244
    Bookmarking Pages 244
    Revisiting Bookmarked & Favourite Sites 246
    Organising Bookmarks 247
    Reading List 248
    Downloads 248
    Extensions 249
    Privacy Reports 250
    Passwords 251
    Managing Passwords 252

Generate Automatic Strong Passwords................253
Autofill Forms 254
Apple Mail................255
Email Threads 256
Show BCC Field................257
Replying to a Message................258
Forward a Message................259
Writing a New Email................260
Formatting your Message................260
Add an Emoji................261
Add Attachment 261
Add Photo from Photos App................262
Mail Drop 262
Mail Markup 264
Dealing with Spam & Junk Mail................266
Contacts 267
Creating Groups 269
Add Email Contact from Apple Mail 270
Facetime 271
Placing Video Calls................271
Calling Someone New................272
Answering Calls 273
Group FaceTime................274
Message App 275
Sending New Messages................275
Sending Files 276
Memojis 277
Message Effects................278
Air Drop................279
From Finder 279
In Safari................280
Mac Phone 281
Using Multimedia................282
Photos App................283
Importing your Photos................284
Manipulating & Adjusting Photos................286
Adding Filters 289
Creating Folders and Albums................290
Adding Photos to Albums 292
Places 293
Faces 295
Memories 298
Create your Own Memory................298
Smart Search 301
Sharing Photos 302

Shared Albums...303
Printing Photos...305
Creating Slideshows..307
Printing & Publishing Photos..309
Installing the Apps..309
Creating Photobooks...310
Ordering Prints 314
Greeting Cards 316
Continuity Camera..318
Insert Photo from iPhone/iPad 318
Add Sketch 320
Scan a Document..321
iMovie 322
Importing Footage from your Camera...................................322
Importing Footage from your iPhone....................................323
Adding Clips..325
Adding Titles 326
Adding Music...327
Transitions...328
Animations 329
Music App...330
Subscribing to Apple Music 330
The Main Screen...331
Searching for Music...332
Add to Library 333
Creating Playlists 334
Importing CDs..335
Adding Tracks to your iPhone, or iPad Manually 336
Burning CDs 338
Podcasts App 339
iTunes Store..341
Apple TV App 343
Watch Now 343
Searching for Media...344
Library..345
Apple TV+ Streaming...346
Airplay 347
Cancelling Subscriptions..349

Maintaining your Mac **350**

Firewalls 351
Enabling the Firewall 351
Firewall Settings...352
Do Apple Macs get Viruses? 353
Downloading MacOS Big Sur..355
Installing MacOS Big Sur 356

Create a Boot Drive 357
Booting from a USB Drive 361
Internet Restore 365
Recovery Mode 366
App Updates 366
System Updates 367
Mac Storage Management 368
Disk Utility... 370
    Checking Drives...*371*
    Formatting Drives *371*
    Partitioning Drives *373*
FileVault 375
Encrypt External Drive... 376
Decrypt External Drive... 376
Reset SMC 377
    New Macbooks (2018+) *377*
    Older Macbooks..*378*
    iMac, Mac Pro and Mac Mini..............................*378*
Reset NVRAM 379

Video Resources **380**

Index **384**

About the Author

With over 15 years' experience in the computer industry, Kevin Wilson has made a career out of technology and showing others how to use it. After earning a master's degree in computer science, software engineering, and multimedia systems, Kevin has held various positions in the IT industry including graphic & web design, building & managing corporate networks, training, and IT support.

He currently serves as Elluminet Press LTD's senior writer and director, he periodically teaches computer science at college in South Africa and serves as an IT trainer in England. His books have become a valuable resource among the students in England, South Africa and our partners in the United States.

Kevin's motto is clear: "If you can't explain something simply, then you haven't understood it well enough." To that end, he has created the Computer Fundamentals Series, in which he breaks down complex technological subjects into smaller, easy-to-follow steps that students and ordinary computer users can put into practice.

Acknowledgements

Thanks to all the staff at Luminescent Media & Elluminet Press for their passion, dedication and hard work in the preparation and production of this book.

To all my friends and family for their continued support and encouragement in all my writing projects.

To all my colleagues, students and testers who took the time to test procedures and offer feedback on the book

Finally thanks to you the reader for choosing this book. I hope it helps you to use your mac with greater understanding.

Have fun!

MacOS Big Sur

Named after the rugged region of the Central Coast of California, MacOS Big Sur moves to version 11.0, and is the seventeenth major release of Apple's desktop operating system for Macintosh computers.

According to Apple, the following Macs will be able to run MacOS Big Sur:

- MacBook (2015 and later)
- MacBook Air (2013 and later)
- MacBook Pro (Late 2013 and later)
- Mac mini (2014 and later)
- iMac (2014 and later)
- iMac Pro (2017 and later)
- Mac Pro (2013 and later)

Keep this in mind if you're upgrading from a previous version of MacOS.

What's New?

Version 11 introduces a revamped user interface. Windows now have a curved design around the edges with a lighter, more spacious look.

The dock has been moved off the bottom of the screen and the icons have a more uniform curved shape, similar to that found on an iPhone or iPad.

Control Center has been redesigned to incorporate menu bar items into a single place giving you instant access to commonly used controls such as wi-fi, bluetooth devices, display brightness and volume.

Notification Center puts all your notifications and widgets into a single place.

There are also new widgets for Calendar, Stocks, Weather, Reminders, Notes, and Podcasts.

Chapter 1: MacOS Big Sur

The menu bar along the top of the screen is translucent, and menus are a bit larger with more space separating the commands making them easier to read.

Safari has had a few improvements. There is a new start page you can customise, launch your favourite sites, see frequently visited websites and check your reading list.

A new dedicated category in the App Store makes it easy to find and install extensions in Safari.

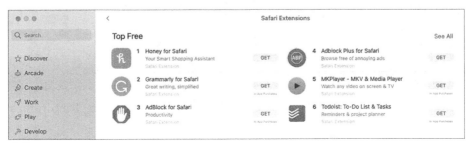

With the redesigned Maps App you can create guides, discover new places, find indoor maps, and share them with friends and family.

You can also explore certain cities in 3D with the 'look around' feature.

System sounds have been updated with new system alerts that sound familiar. Software updates now download in the background and complete faster than before.

Also various other minor changes. You'll find a full list on Apple's website.

www.apple.com/macos/big-sur/features/

Available Macs

Let's take a closer look at the different Macs available from the Apple Store.

Macbook Air

The Macbook Air is great for an on-the-go lifestyle as they are small and light, but is only suited to basic computing such as internet browsing, email, photos, music, messages, facetime, and so on.

Macbook Pro

The Macbook Pro offers more processing power, is aimed at creative types and those who use more power-hungry apps such as games, video editing, music production, graphic design, and so on.

iMac

The iMac is Apple's 'all in one' desktop computer and comes in two different sizes. All iMacs come with keyboard and mouse. These are great for the average user and can run a variety of power hungry apps as well as internet, email, facetime, etc.

iMac Pro

The iMac Pro is similar to the iMac, except the iMac Pro has much faster processor and comes with an SSD drive. The iMac Pro is a dark grey colour instead of the silver on the iMac.

These machines are aimed at creative types and power users and are very fast. They are well suited to video editing, graphic design, and music production.

Mac Pro

The Mac Pro is a rather unique looking machine and is the most powerful of the Mac computers. This machine does not come with a screen, nor a keyboard and mouse - so you'll need to buy these separately.

These machines are aimed at creative types and power users and are very fast. They are well suited to video editing, graphic design, and music production.

Mac Mini

The idea behind the Mac Mini was to allow users to use their existing screen, keyboard, and mouse. It's worth noting that you will need a screen that connects to the computer using an HDMI cable.

If your screen uses VGA or DVI, you'll need an adapter to convert to HDMI.

Setting up Your Mac

In this chapter, we'll take a look at setting up your Mac from powering up, running the initial setup, to setting up WiFi connections, adding email accounts, printers, and time machine backup.

We'll also take a look at managing fonts, configuring your system, and pairing bluetooth devices.

To help you better understand this section, take a look at the video resources. Open your web browser and type the following URL into the address field at the top of the window:

```
videos.tips/using-sur
```

Upgrading to Big Sur

To update your mac, open the system preferences (see page 47 on how to open system preferences). Select 'software update'.

If there are any updates available, they will be listed here. Click 'update now' to apply the updates.

Select 'automatically keep my mac up to date' and MacOS will automatically apply the updates in the background. Click 'advanced' to select which updates to apply automatically.

Select them all, then click 'ok'. This will ensure your mac is always up to date and it will do this in the background without prompting you.

Chapter 2: Setting up Your Mac

If you don't see any updates, you can check on Apple's website. Open Safari and navigate to the following website

`www.apple.com/macos/how-to-upgrade`

Click 'upgrade now' on the top right of the web page.

The macOS Big Sur update will open up in the app store. Click 'get' on the top right to start the upgrade.

Click 'download' on the confirmation prompt.

The update will start to download. This can take a while.

Your mac will restart to apply the update. Again this will take a while. Once the update is complete, you'll be running macOS Big Sur.

Power Up

The power button on the mac is on the top right of the keyboard on a Macbook Air and Macbook Pro.

 or

On the Mac Pro, you'll find the power button on the top panel.

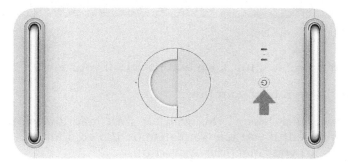

On the iMac and Mac Mini, the power button is situated on the back panel.

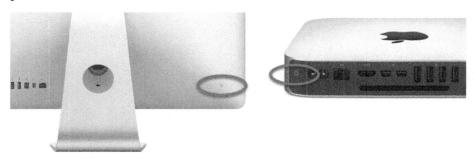

Press the button once to start up your mac.

You can also use the power button to force your mac to shutdown in the event of a crash or lock up. Hold the button until the screen goes blank. Only use this option if you're having problems.

Power Down

To power down your mac or send it into sleep/standby mode, go to the apple menu on the top left of the screen...'

From the menu...

Click 'shut down' to shut down and power off your mac.

Click 'restart' to reboot your mac.

You can also click 'sleep', this will put your mac into standby mode and is convenient if you use your mac on the go a lot and don't have time to wait for your machine to start up.

If you are using a macbook laptop, you can just close the lid and your macbook will go into sleep mode.

Starting your Mac for the First Time

When you turn on a new mac for the first time, you'll need to go through some initial steps to set up WiFi, select language, regional preferences and sign in with your Apple ID.

To begin, select your country of residence. Click 'continue'.

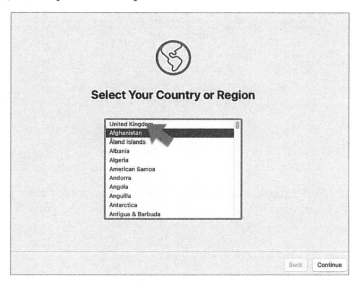

Tap 'continue' on the 'written and spoken languages' page.

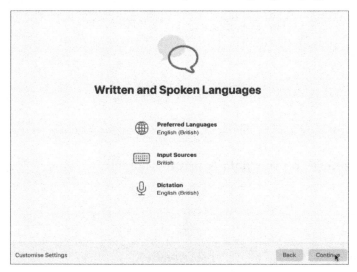

If the language settings aren't correct, tap 'customise settings'.

Chapter 2: Setting up Your Mac

Click 'not now' on the accessibility screen. You can configure these later in the settings app if you need to make any changes according to your needs.

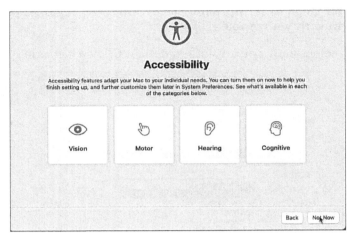

Select your WiFi network and enter your password when prompted. Your Wi-Fi password is usually printed on the back of your WiFi router.

Click 'continue' on the 'data & privacy' screen.

Click 'not now' on the 'migration assistant' screen. You can transfer data from an old machine later.

Sign in with your Apple ID email address and password. Click 'continue'.

You may be prompted to enter a verification code. This code will be sent to another Apple device such as your iPhone or iPad. On your iPad or iPhone tap 'allow', then copy the code into the boxes on your Mac.

Chapter 2: Setting up Your Mac

Accept the 'terms and conditions', click 'continue'.

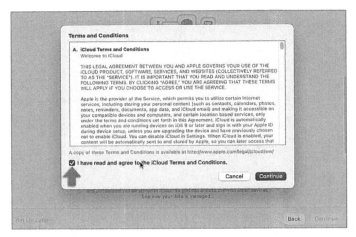

Create your computer account. This is the account you'll use to log into your Mac and it is different from your Apple ID account. Enter a password, then click 'continue'.

Click 'customise settings' on the 'express setup' screen.

Enable location services. It is safe to enable this and it will allow you to make use of location based services such as maps, local news, and weather. Click 'enable location services on this mac', then click 'continue'.

Click 'continue' on the 'analytics' screen

Click 'continue' on the 'screen time' page.

Enable Siri, click 'continue'.

Then on the next screen, click 'not now', click 'continue'.

If you're using a macbook with a finger print scanner, you will be asked to set up your finger prints so you can log into your Mac. Click 'continue' and follow the instructions to register your finger print.

Select your look. You can choose from light mode or dark mode. Dark mode is good for low light conditions and night time viewing. It removes most of the bright white colour from the screen. Click 'light' or 'dark', or select 'auto' to use light mode during the day, and dark mode during the evening.

Give your Mac a few minutes to complete the setup.

You'll land on the desktop when the setup finishes.

Now you can start to use your Mac.

31

Apple ID

Your Apple ID contains all your personal information, messages, calendar, contacts, email, and various settings.

Create a New ID

To create an Apple ID open safari and go to the following website:

`appleid.apple.com`

From the website click 'Create your Apple ID' on the top right.

Fill in the form with your details, scroll down to the bottom and click 'continue'.

Keep a note of the email address and password you entered. You will need this Apple ID if you want to purchase Apps from the App Store, use iCloud, Apple Email, or purchase songs from iTunes Store.

iCloud

iCloud is a cloud storage service developed by Apple. iCloud enables you to store your email, messages, documents, photos, and music on Apple's remote servers. This enables you to share data between your devices and with other users.

If you haven't signed in, go to system preferences, click 'apple id' and enter your Apple ID username and password.

From here you can change your iCloud settings. Use the panel on the left hand side to navigate between the sections.

Select 'name, phone, email' to change iCloud password, or your name. To change your password, click 'password & security'. To add payment methods, select 'payment & shipping.

iCloud Drive Setup

Go to system preferences, click 'apple id' and enter your Apple ID username and password if prompted.

Select 'icloud' from the panel on the left.

To change which apps store documents on data on iCloud, click 'options' next to 'iCloud Drive'.

Select your apps you want to use iCloud Drive. Click 'done'.

iCloud Sync

Go to system preferences, select 'apple id', then click 'icloud' on the left had side of the window. Here, you can select which apps you want to synchronise across all your devices.

Click the tick next to the app name to turn on and off.

Storage Management

iCloud Storage Management allows you to manage what data is saved on your iCloud Storage. To manage your iCloud storage, go to system preferences, select 'apple id', then click 'icloud'.

At the bottom of the window, you'll see a chart showing a breakdown of the space used on your iCloud Storage. Click 'manage'.

Here, you'll see a more detailed breakdown of the apps using storage on iCloud and the amount of space they've taken up. Now the data stored on iCloud isn't the app itself, it's the data such as your messages, photos you've taken, device backups etc.

Click on the app to view details and delete any data. This is useful if your iCloud storage is running low.

Click 'buy more storage' if you need more than 5GB of iCloud storage. There is a charge for larger storage plans.

Setup Internet

There are various ways to connect to the internet, the most common being WiFi. You can also connect using an ethernet cable.

WiFi

To set up your WiFi, select the WiFi symbol on the status menu on the right hand side of the screen. From the drop down, click 'other networks'. Select the network you want to connect to (SSID).

In the dialog box that appears on your screen, enter the WiFi password (sometimes called a network key).

On a home network, your WiFi password is usually printed on the back of your modem, access point, or router.

If you don't see the WiFi icon on the top right, go to system preferences and select 'network'. Click 'WiFi' on the left hand side of the window, then click 'network name'. From the drop down box, select the network you want to connect to.

Using an Ethernet Cable

If WiFi isn't available, and you use a cable modem to get online in your home, you can use a cable.

Here is a typical setup.

Your coax cable coming into your home is usually split using a splitter. One cable will go to your TV and the other will go to your modem.

Your computer will connect to your modem using an Ethernet cable.

Plug one end of the Ethernet cable into your modem, then power up your modem and allow it to connect to your ISP.

Plug the other end into the Ethernet port on your computer, as shown below.

Chapter 2: Setting up Your Mac

Your mac should connect automatically. To check, go to system preferences.

Select 'network' from the preferences.

Click on Ethernet on the left hand side, and make sure IPv4 is set to DHCP and your computer has picked up an IP address.

Phone Tethering

Tethering allows you to share your iPhone's data connection with your Mac. To set this up, on your iPhone go to the settings app and tap 'personal hotspot'. Toggle 'personal hotspot' to on, then enable your bluetooth.

On your Mac, your iPhone appears in the WiFi menu as another network.

In this example the iPhone is called 'iPhoneAPC3', so I'd select that one from the WiFi networks.

When prompted on your Mac, enter the WiFi password shown in the personal hotspot settings on your iPhone, as show above.

Mobile USB Modems

If you use your Mac on the go a lot or travel frequently, you should also consider using 3G/4G/5G LTE mobile data modem. You can get these from a phone provider such as AT&T, Verizon, o2, T-Mobile, etc.

When you buy these from your phone provider, you can take out a contract or pay as you go in the same way you'd buy a cell/mobile phone.

You'll need to follow the instructions from your phone supplier for specifics. However the procedure is very similar.

You'll usually need to install a piece of software to manage your device.

Plug your dongle into a USB port on your Mac.

Double click the icon that appears on your desktop.

Open the folder called 'Mac' if there is one, then double-click the setup package. Follow the instructions on screen.

Once installed you can use the connection manager to connect to your service.

Virtual Private Networks

A Virtual Private Network (or VPN) is a secure connection where data is send and received over the internet through an encrypted tunnel. This means you can browse the internet anonymously and your data is safe on unsecured networks such as public WiFi.

Using a VPN Service

There are various different VPN services available. Eg Windscribe. Windscribe is a good starter service as you get 10GB of free data a month. To use the service, you'll need to download the app. Go to:

```
windscribe.com/download
```

Scroll down, click the 'mac' icon under 'windscribe for your computer'.

Click the downloads icon on the top right of Safari, from the drop down double click the download to begin.

Follow the on screen instructions to sign up and activate the service. You'll find the VPN app on launch pad - click to start the app if it isn't already running. Click the icon on the top right of the screen. In the drop down window, click the switch on the top left to turn on the VPN.

Manual Setup

Open the preferences app then select 'network'. Click the '+' icon on the bottom left

In the 'interface' drop down, select 'VPN'. Then in 'VPN type' select the kind of VPN connection you want to set up. Get this info from your VPN service or Administrator. Give the connection a name, click 'create'.

Enter the server address and the remote ID for the VPN connection. Get this info from your VPN service or administrator.

Server Address:	vpn.elluminetpress.com
Remote ID:	vpn.elluminetpress.com
Local ID:	

Authentication Settings...

Click 'authentication settings'. In the drop down box, select method of authentication: username or certificate. Get this info from your VPN service or administrator.

Authentication Settings:

Username

Username:	username
Password:	••••••••

Cancel   OK

Click 'ok'. Click 'advanced', under the DNS tab, click the '+' on the bottom left and enter a DNS server address.

Connecting Peripherals

You can connect peripherals such as external drives, scanners, and printers. You connect peripherals using a USB cable. On the side panel of the MacBook, you'll find your USB ports. These will be USB-C ports. On the side panel of your macbook, you'll see these ports.

If you need standard USB ports, or HDMI, then you can get a hub that plugs into the side of your macbook.

These USB-C hubs are available at most computer stores and online.

The USB-C hub will allow you to use the USB-A type used on the most common peripherals.

Chapter 2: Setting up Your Mac

On the back panel of the iMac. Here you'll see your USB ports, ethernet, headphones, and an SD card reader so you can read memory cards from digital cameras.

The back panel of your mac mini 2018. Here you'll find your USB ports, and HDMI port for plugging in a monitor, ethernet, and a headphone jack.

You'll also find the power buttons and power cable ports.

System Preferences

System preferences is the control panel for your mac. Here you can personalise your system and change settings.

To open your system preferences, click the Apple menu on the top left hand side of your screen, and select 'system preferences'.

Chapter 2: Setting up Your Mac

Here is a brief explanation of what each of the sections in the system preferences panel does and where to go when you are looking for a setting.

Option	Description
Apple ID	Configure iCloud settings, media & purchases, Apple ID account details, manage iCloud storage, and family settings
Family Sharing	Manage and monitor your child's activity when using your mac
General	Changes to the general colour scheme, light/dark mode, scroll bars, default browser.
Desktop & Screen Saver	Change desktop pictures as well as screen saver settings
Dock	Dock size, location, and effects
Mission Control	Configure hot corners, mission control keyboard and mouse shortcuts, as well as launch pad
Siri	Configure, Enable/disable Siri
Spotlight	Preferences for system wide search settings
Language & Region	Set language, regional settings for on screen text, calendar, time formats, as well as keyboard layout preferences
Notifications	Notification center settings, alerts, banners and which apps are allowed send notifications.
Internet Accounts	Add email accounts
Users & Groups	Add and delete mac user accounts, change mac passwords, auto login or user switching
Accessibility	Manage screen readability, voice over, speech, etc
Screen Time	Configure screen time, monitor usage, block apps and websites
Extensions	Add third party extensions to photos, actions, finder, share menu etc
Security & Preferences	File vault drive encryption, gatekeeper, firewall and privacy settings. Password change for current user
Software Update	MacOS system updates
Network	Network settings for WiFi, ethernet. Adjust IP addresses, TCP/IP, DNS, proxy servers, VPNs
Bluetooth	Pair bluetooth devices. Turn on/off bluetooth.
Sound	Set system sound effects, microphone or speaker settings
Printers & Scanners	Add printers or scanner devices, as well as device settings
Keyboard	Set keyboard shortcuts, keyboard country layout settings & dictation
Trackpad	Set pointer track speed and sensitivity, as well as multi touch gestures
Mouse	Set pointer track speed, scroll speed and double click speed
Displays	Set display resolution, colour calibration, and multiple screen settings
Energy Saver	Set sleep times for screen, system and disk drives
Date & Time	Set date and time format for different locations, time zones, etc
Sharing	Share files or a printer attached to your mac. Remote login, screen sharing and internet sharing settings.
Time Machine	Time machine settings to back up files to an external hard disk
Startup Disk	Select disk macos uses to boot from

Whenever you need to change a setting or a preference you should come to the system preferences panel.

Add a Printer

Click on the Apple menu on the top left of your screen. From this menu, select 'System Preferences'.

From the system preferences window, double click 'Printers & Scanners'.

Click on the plus sign shown below to add a printer.

Chapter 2: Setting up Your Mac

In the box that appears, MacOS will scan for connected printers; whether they are connected via USB or WiFi.

Select your printer from the 'use' list if necessary, then click 'add'. Your mac will download the driver from its own driver library.

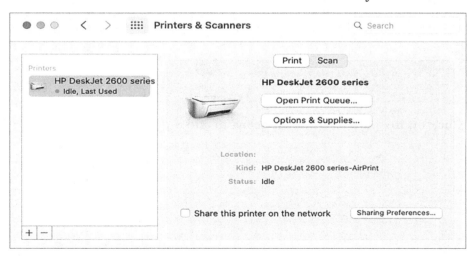

Have a look at the printer demos at: videos.tips/using-sur

Connect Printer to WiFi

Nowadays you'd connect your printer to your Mac using WiFi. It is difficult to give specific instructions on printer setup as each model of printer and each manufacturer has its own method. However, I will provide some general guidelines you can use to get started.

If your printer is brand new, you'll need to connect it to your Wifi. Printers with LCD panels display step-by-step instructions for setting up the wireless connection when you first turn on the printer. So read the instructions for specifics on how to do this.

If your printer doesn't have an LCD panel, use the WPS method. You can use this method if you have a WPS button on your router - as shown in the photo below. Refer to the printer's quick start guide to find the exact procedure for your printer model. Usually you have to press and hold the WiFi button on your printer for a few seconds, then go to your router and press the WPS button.

If your router doesn't have a WPS button, you'll have to select your WiFi network (SSID) and enter your WiFi password on your printer. You'll need to refer to the printer's instructions on exactly how to do that on your particular printer.

Other Email Accounts

You can add all your email accounts such as Gmail, Yahoo, Microsoft and any email accounts you may have. To to this, open system preferences.

From the system preferences, select 'internet accounts'.

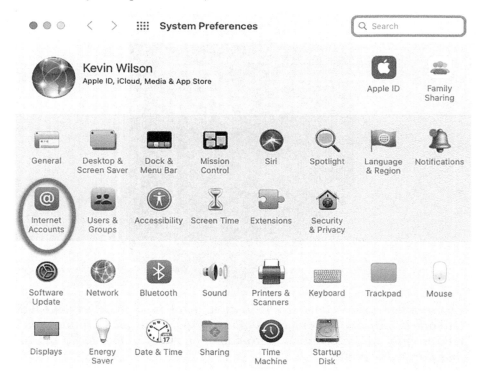

To add an account, tap the icon on the right had side.

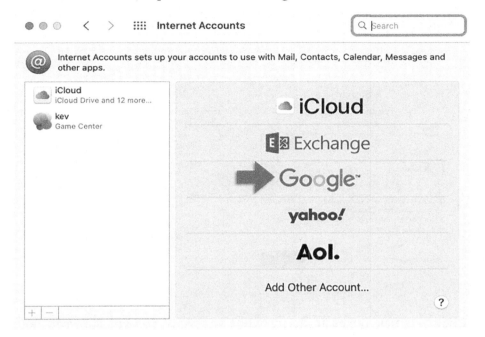

If you have a Gmail account, click 'google'. If you have a Microsoft Account use 'exchange'. For yahoo mail select 'yahoo'. For any other email account click 'add other account' at the bottom of the list.

In this example, I'm adding my Gmail account. So I'd click 'google'.

Click 'open browser' on the popup prompt.

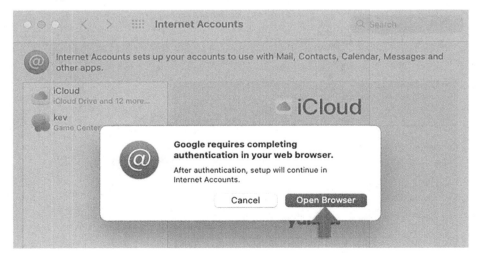

Sign in with your Gmail email address and password. Click 'next'. On the next screen click 'allow' to give macOS permission to access your Gmail account.

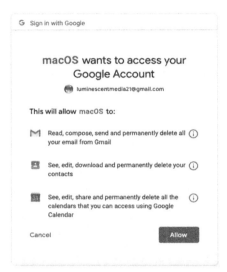

Click the tick boxes to select what you want to sync between your mac and your Gmail account. You can bring over your email, contacts, calendars and notes. All these will be added to your mail, contacts, calendar, and notes apps on your mac.

Click 'done' when you're finished.

Additional Users

You can create multiple user accounts for all those who use your Mac. So you could create one for each family member.

To do this, open the system preferences. Click the Apple menu on the top left, then select 'system preferences'

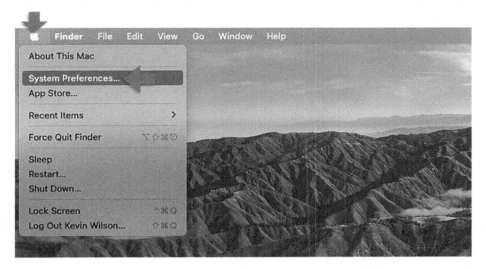

Click 'users & groups' from the 'system preferences' window.

Click the small padlock on the bottom left of the window to unlock the settings. Enter your mac username and password - the one you used to sign into your mac.

To add a new user, click the '+' sign on the bottom left.

Fill in the details in the 'new user' form.

For 'new account', set it to 'standard'. Only use 'administrator' if you want to allow this user to change system settings or install apps.

Enter the user's first and second names into the 'full name' field. Your mac will automatically create an account name.

Enter a password for this account in the 'password' and then again in the 'verify' fields.

Click 'create user' when you're done.

Login Options

To do this, open the system preferences. Click the Apple menu on the top left, then select 'system preferences'

Click 'users & groups' from the 'system preferences' window.

Click the small padlock on the bottom left of the window to unlock the settings. Enter your mac username and password.

Select 'login options' on the bottom left.

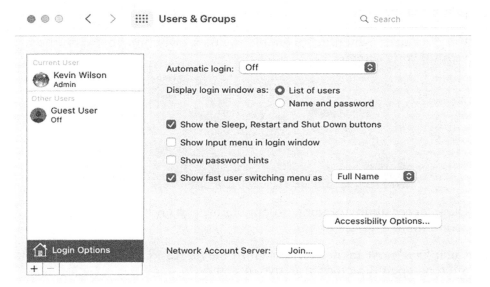

With 'automatic login', you can select an account to automatically log in when you start your Mac.

With 'display login window as', you can display the login screen with a list of registered users or just a username and password field.

With 'sleep, restart and shutdown buttons' you can choose whether to display these along the bottom of the login screen or not.

With 'show input menu in login screen' you can show or hide the input icon on the top right of the login screen.

'Show password hints' shows your hint when you mistype your password.

Use 'fast user switching' to enable the user switching menu on the top right of your screen.

Click 'accessibility options' to enable on screen keyboard, voice over, zoom, mouse keys, etc.

Click 'join' next to 'network account server' to join a network domain such as open directory or active directory.

Change Passwords

You can change your mac password and your Apple ID password from the system preferences.

Mac Password

To change your mac password - the password you use to unlock your mac, click the Apple menu on the top left, then select 'system preferences' from the menu.

Select 'users & groups' from the system preferences window.

Select the 'password' tab, then click 'change password'.

In the dialog box that appears, enter your current password in the 'old password' field, then enter your new password into the 'new password' and 'verify' fields. Click 'change password' to confirm.

Chapter 2: Setting up Your Mac

Apple ID Password

To change your mac password - the password you use to sign into your Apple ID, App Store, etc, click the Apple menu on the top left, then select 'system preferences' from the menu.

Click your Apple ID account at the top of the preferences window.

Click 'password & security' on the left hand side.

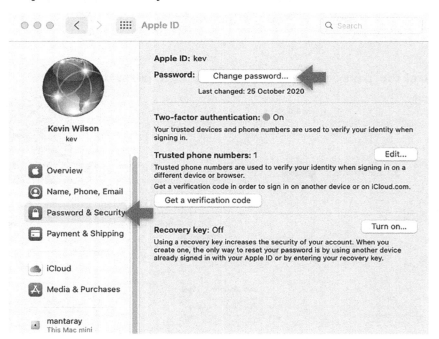

Click 'change password'. In the popup dialog box, enter your new password.

Setup Apple Pay

To set up Apple Pay, go to the settings app on your iPhone, scroll down and tap 'wallet & apple pay'. Then tap 'add card'.

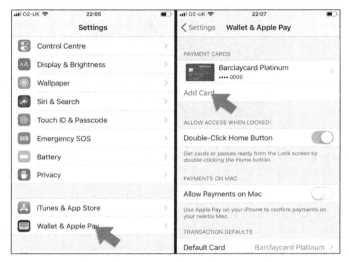

If you already have a credit/debit card registered with your Apple ID, then apple pay will ask you to add this one.

If this is the card you want to use, then enter the 3 digit security code and tap 'next' on the top right. Hit 'agree' on the terms and conditions. Your card will be added.

If you want to add a different card, tap 'add a different card' underneath.

Position the card so it fills the white rectangle on your screen. Apple Pay will scan your card and automatically enter your details

If you can't get the camera to scan the card, tap 'enter card details manually' then key in your card number, exp dates, and so on.

Tap next. Check and confirm your card details. Make any changes if necessary, so the details match those on your card. Tap next, then tap 'agree' to the terms and conditions.

Now you'll need to verify your card. Some banks use different methods, so read the instructions on the screen. In this example, the bank will send a code via SMS to the phone number registered when the bank account was opened. Tap 'next'.

Check your SMS messages and enter the verification code in the field. Tap 'next'.

Setup Apple Pay on a Macbook

If your Macbook has a touch sensor on the top right of they keyboard, then you can use this method to set up apple pay. Open system preferences and select 'wallet & apple pay'.

Tap 'add card' on the bottom right

Point the front of your card at your camera. Position your card in the white rectangle. Allow your mac to identify the card. Click 'next'.

Check and amend any details if necessary. Enter your 3 digit security code. Click 'next'. Your bank will verify your information. After your bank has verified your card you can use apple pay.

You'll be able to edit your contact and shipping info, see card details and add new cards on the 'details' tab. You'll also be able to see a transaction history on the 'transactions' tab

Touch ID

You can use Touch ID on a mac that has a touch sensor such as a macbook air or macbook pro.

Click the Apple menu on the top left, then select 'system preferences'

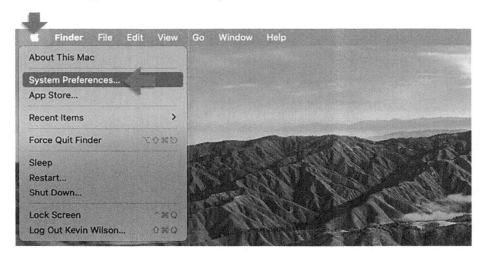

Click 'touch id' from the 'system preferences' window.

Select all items under 'use touch id for'. Click 'add a fingerprint'.

Now scan the finger you most likely use to turn on your mac - eg index finger.

Place Your Finger

Lift and rest your finger on Touch ID repeatedly.

Cancel

Rest your finger on the touch sensor, remove your finger, then rest your finger on the sensor again. You'll need to do this multiple times until your Mac tells you the procedure is complete.

Once complete, click 'done'.

Touch ID Is Ready

Your fingerprint can be used to unlock your Mac.

Done

You'll now be able to unlock your mac with Touch ID, use apple pay to pay for things on the web, or Apple Store.

Dark Mode & Light Mode

Dark mode allows you to change the look of the interface to tackle the problem of eye strain when using a computer in low light conditions or for long periods of time.

To enable dark mode, open your system preferences and select 'general'. Change the 'appearance' option to 'dark'. *You can also set the appearance mode to 'auto'. This means you'll get light mode during daylight hours and dark mode at night.*

Dark Mode is designed to put less strain on the eyes and is intended to make reading a computer screen easier. Here in the screen shot below you can dark mode on the left and light mode on the right. Dark mode has a high contrast visual look with dark backgrounds and white text.

The dock along the bottom also shows up in a dark colour showing up the icons a lot clearer.

Setup your Trackpad

Personally I find the default settings on the trackpad to be very unresponsive and hard to use. So I tweak the settings in the system preferences.

Open your system preferences. Click the Apple menu on the top left, then select 'system preferences' from the menu.

Select 'trackpad' from the system preferences window.

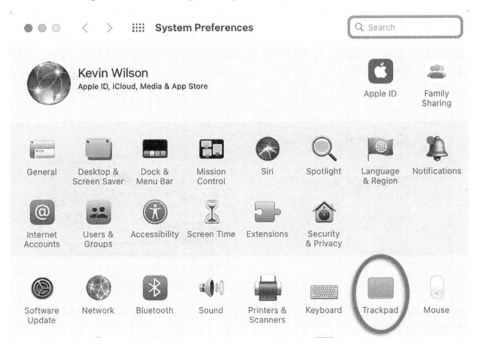

On the point and click tab, enable 'tap to click'. This allows you to use the tap feature to select something, rather than trying to click the left button on the trackpad.

Also turn up the tracking speed if you find the mouse pointer really slow.

On the 'scroll & zoom' tab, un-check 'scroll direction: natural'. So when you run your fingers down the trackpad your page scrolls down with you instead of up.

This makes it a lot easier to navigate through pages on websites and other applications.

Setup your Mouse

Personally I find the default settings on the mouse to be very unresponsive and hard to use. So I tweak the settings in the system preferences.

Open your system preferences. Click the Apple menu on the top left, then select 'system preferences' from the menu.

Select 'mouse' from the system preferences window.

Remove the tick from 'scroll direction: natural', so your pages move in the right direction when you scroll up and down.

Increase the 'tracking speed' until you have the desired mouse pointer speed when you move the mouse. This will make it less strenuous on your wrist.

If you have a bluetooth mouse, see "Pairing Bluetooth Devices" on page 78.

Screensavers

Open your system preferences. Click the Apple menu on the top left, then select 'system preferences' from the menu. Then select 'desktop & screensaver' from the system preferences window.

Select the screensaver tab. Here, you can select a screensaver, set the length of time before the screensaver appears - to do this click the drop down box next to 'start after', select a time. I find it best to turn off the screensavers, since your machine goes into sleep mode.

Dynamic Desktop

With dynamic desktops, wallpapers change according to the time of day, meaning they change the lighting and look of the wallpaper image during the day.

In the afternoon, the wallpaper is at its brightest, and at night, the sky in the wallpaper shifts to darker blue to reflect the evening. This helps to adapt the screen look and brightness to the changing ambient light levels during the day.

To adjust your wallpapers, right click on the desktop and select 'change desktop background'.

At the top you'll see 'Big Sur' and 'dynamic' in the selection box. This means the desktop will change during the course of the day. Select 'desktop pictures' then select a dynamic desktop.

Desktop Wallpaper

You can change the background image on your desktop to anything you like. Perhaps a loved one? Child? Or a picture from your last vacation, or outing with a friend? You can use a photograph taken from your iPhone or iPad. To do this, open the photos app on your mac.

Double click the photo you want to use.

Click the share icon on the top right, then select 'set desktop picture'.

Your picture will appear on your desktop.

Managing Displays

You can manage the displays you connect to your mac. You can also connect multiple displays to your mac. This could be another monitor, projector or TV.

Open your system preferences. Click the Apple menu on the top left, then select 'system preferences' from the menu.

Select 'displays' from the system preferences window.

From the 'display' tab, you can set the resolution for your particular display. Note, macOS usually sets most of these things automatically, but you can change them from here if you need to.

Select 'default for this display' to set the best settings. If you need to change the resolution, select 'scaled' and select the desired resolution from the popup list.

You can also rotate your screen. Set to 'standard' for normal wide screen.

The 'arrangement' tab appears when you have more than one display connected to your mac. Here, you can configure which display is your primary monitor. You can also arrange your displays. Each display connected to your mac is represented with a blue rectangle. Your main display is marked with a white line along the top.

Arrange the rectangles to match the physical arrangement of your displays. So for example, my second display is on the left hand side of my main display - as shown below.

The blue rectangles in the 'arrangement' tab match the physical arrangement.

This makes it easier to drag apps, files or folders to your second display while you're working.

From the colour tab, you can set the colour profile for your particular display. MacOS will normally select the best colour profile for your display, however you can select another one here.

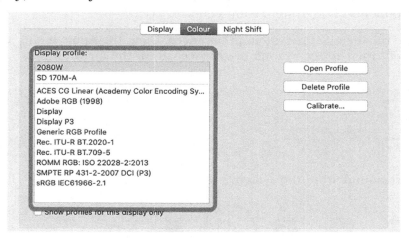

You can also calibrate your display. This is useful if you do a lot of graphic design or photography. To do this, click 'calibrate' and follow the on screen prompts and instructions.

Night shift, removes the blue light to make it easier on your eyes. To turn it on, click the drop down box next to 'schedule', select 'sunset to sunrise' to enable night shift mode in the evenings.

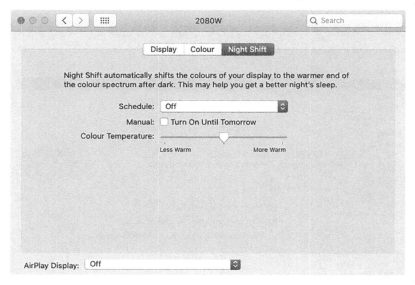

Select 'custom' from the drop down box to set your own times.

System Audio

You can manage your audio devices such as external speaker systems, microphones, and system sound effects.

To do this open your system preferences. Click the Apple menu on the top left, then select 'system preferences' from the menu.

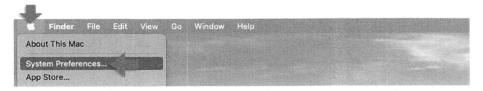

Select 'sound' from the system preferences window.

Click the 'sound effects' tab. Here you can select a sound to play for system alerts, select the audio device to play the sounds through, alter alert volume, play a sound when you start your mac, enable/disable system interface sound effects, play a sound when you change the volume and adjust the main system volume.

You can manage the audio output devices, such as headphones and speaker systems, as well as the internal speakers on your mac. To do this click the 'output' tab. Select the one you want to send audio to.

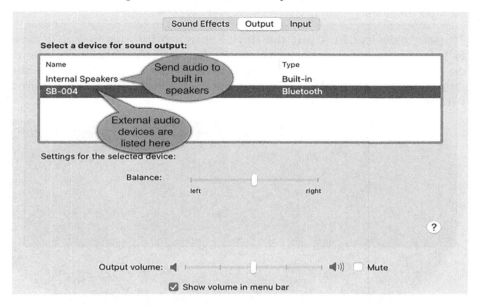

The 'input' tab lists all your audio input devices such as a microphones and any 'line in' device that is connected to your mac. Select your mic.

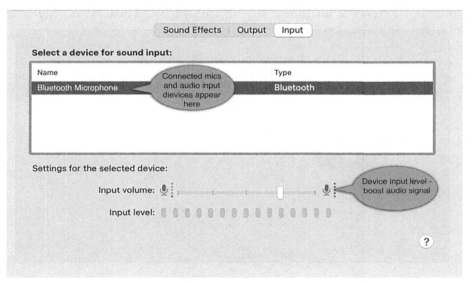

Talk into the mic, if it is working correctly you'll see the 'input level' spike as you talk.

Pairing Bluetooth Devices

You can pair bluetooth keyboards, headphones, and most bluetooth capable devices.

To pair a device, first put the device into pairing mode. You'll need to refer to the device's instructions to find specific details on how to do this. On most devices, press and hold the pairing button until the status light starts flashing. This means the device is ready to be paired with your Mac.

On your Mac, open the system preferences app. From the app, select 'bluetooth'. On the left hand side of the window click 'turn bluetooth on', if it isn't already.

The bluetooth device will appear in the list. Click 'connect'.

Fonts

You can manage fonts installed on your mac, and install new ones. To see all your fonts, open launchpad and click on 'font book'. If it isn't there, look in the 'other' folder.

From here you can install new fonts and see samples of fonts already installed on your mac.

Chapter 2: Setting up Your Mac

You can download countless fonts from the internet such as `dafont. com`, `fontsquirrel.com`, `myfonts.com`, and so on. To install fonts you've downloaded, drag and drop the font files (.TTF, .OTF and .FON) from finder to 'all fonts' in fontbook. *Many font files are compressed as a zip file, make sure you double click on the zip file to extract the fonts.*

If drag and drop doesn't work, click the + sign at the top next to 'all fonts', then navigate to the downloads folder where the fonts have been saved. Select the fonts you want to install (use control key to select multiple fonts). Click 'open'.

The font will be available in your apps. Within fontbook, you'll find the installed font under 'user' on the left hand panel. From here, you can test your font, type in a sample and see what it looks like.

Use the slider along the right hand side to change the font size.

Find My

This feature allows you to pinpoint your Mac's location and is quite useful if you have misplaced your Mac or had it stolen.

Setup

First you need to activate it on your Mac. Click the Apple menu on the top left, then select 'system preferences' from the menu. From the system preferences window, select 'apple id'.

Select 'iCloud' on the left hand side.

Scroll down to 'find my mac'. Make sure the tick box is checked. Click 'options', enable both 'find my mac' and 'offline finding'.

Make sure location services is turned on. To do this go back to system preferences and select 'security & privacy'.

Select the 'privacy' tab. Click the small padlock on the bottom left of the window and enter your username and password.

Then click 'enable location services'.

Locating & Taking Action

On any device - iPad, Mac or PC, open your web browser and navigate to:

`www.icloud.com`

Sign in with your Apple ID. Select 'find iPhone' from the iCloud control panel.

You can locate all your Apple devices. Select the name of your device from the drop down menu in the top middle of the screen.

You'll see a green dot appear on the map. This is the current location of your device.

On the right hand side of the screen, you can take action. Here you can click 'play sound' to play an annoying sound on your mac wherever it might be. This helps you to locate it if you've lost it in your house somewhere, or annoy a thief if they have possession of it.

You can also remotely lock your mac to prevent any unauthorised access.

Finally you can erase your mac completely. To remove any personal data that is stored on your machine.

Sharing Locations

You can share your location with friends and family. To share your location, open launchpad, then click the 'find my' app

Select 'share my location' on the bottom left.

Enter the Apple ID or phone number of the person you want to share your location with. Tap 'send'.

Choose to share your location for One Hour, Until End of Day, or Share Indefinitely.

The other person will get a prompt on their device. This will allow them to share their location with you.

Check Someone's Location

Open launchpad, then select the 'find my' app. Select the 'people tab' then click on the person's name.

You should see the person's location appear on the map on your mac. Click the 'i' icon on the name tag to show the person's location information.

Click 'contact' to send the person a message, click 'directions' to see directions to the person's current location, click 'notifications' to add a notification when the person arrives at your location, leaves their location or any other specified location.

Time Machine Backup

The Time Machine allows you to create backups of your files to an external hard drive.

Have a look at the backup demo at: `videos.tips/sur-sys`

Setting Up Backups

To use Time Machine, get yourself an external hard drive. You'll need at least 500GB - 1TB in size. Connect your external hard drive to a USB port as shown below.

Click the Apple menu on the top left, then select 'system preferences' from the menu.

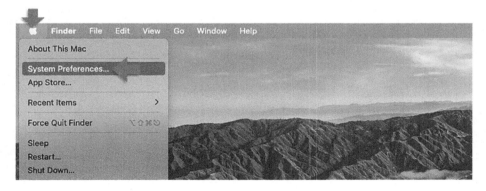

Select 'time machine' from the system preferences window.

Displays   Energy Saver   Date & Time   Sharing   Time Machine   Startup Disk

Chapter 2: Setting up Your Mac

From the time machine window, select 'backup automatically', then click 'select backup disk'.

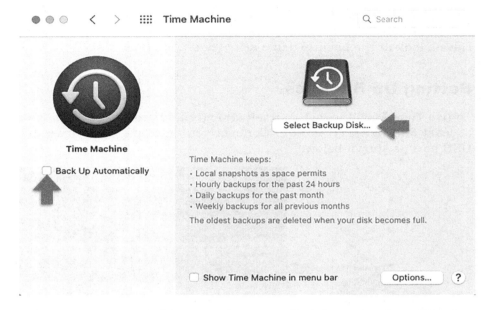

Select your external drive. My drive is called 'Data One', so I'll select that one. The drive is usually labelled with the manufacturer's name or model. Select 'use disk'.

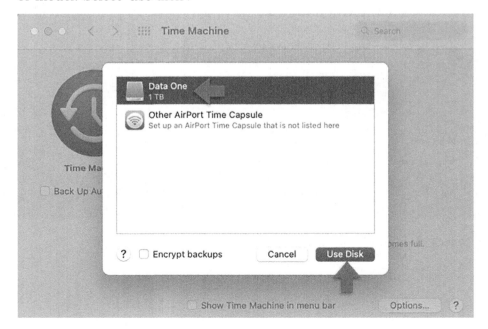

Make sure you use a blank external hard drive and not one that contains any important files. Time Machine will ask you if you want to erase the disk, click 'erase'.

Select 'show time machine in menu bar' on the bottom of the 'time machine' window, to allow you quick access to your backups.

Time Machine will now prepare your external drive for backups and backup your files. This will take a while.

Note, the backup will not work unless the external drive is connected to your Mac. Make sure you connect your hard drive at least weekly, or daily depending on how much work you do.

Whenever you want to back up, just connect your external hard drive and the backup will start automatically.

If not, click the Time Machine icon on the menu bar on the top right and select 'backup now'.

Select 'open time machine preferences' to check. You'll see the backup status in the time machine window.

Restoring Items

To restore something click the icon on your menu bar as shown below.

Plug in your external hard drive you used to back up.

Look for the file in the finder window shown below..

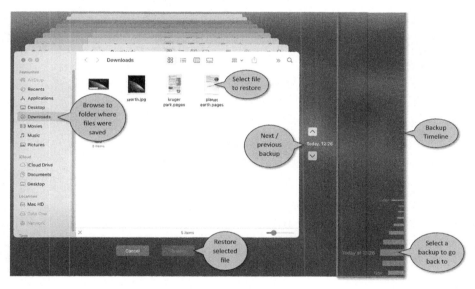

Using the timeline on the right, select what date or time to go back to.

When you have found the file, click restore on the bottom right of the screen. The file will be restored to its original location.

Transfer Files from a Windows PC

If you have used a Windows machine in the past and have moved to a Mac, you can transfer your files using the Windows Migration Assistant.

Before you start, make sure your Mac and PC are connected to the same network (or the same WiFi).

First you need to prepare your PC. You'll need to download the migration assistant. Go to the following website and download the program.

support.apple.com/kb/DL1978

On your PC, run the migration assistant installer in your 'downloads' folder and run through the installation. Once installed, run the migration assistant - you'll find the icon on your desktop. Click 'continue'.

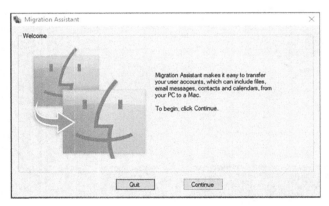

Now when you reach this screen. Go start the migration assistant on your Mac.

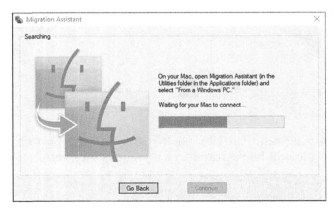

On your Mac start the Migration Assistant. You'll find it in finder -> applications -> utilities. Enter your mac username and password when prompted. Follow the prompts until you get to the migration page. Select 'From a Windows PC', then click Continue.

Click 'continue' to close any other open apps.

On your Mac, select your PC from the list of available computers. Click 'continue'.

When both computers display the same passcode, click 'continue' on your PC and Mac.

Chapter 2: Setting up Your Mac

Your Mac will the drives on your PC and build a list of files to transfer. When the scan is complete, select the files that you want to transfer to your Mac then click 'continue'.

You can watch the progress and estimated time remaining on both the PC and your Mac. This might take a while.

When transfer completes, you'll find a new user account. Set a password, and sign in with your apple id. Run through the setup prompts. You'll find all the files you transferred in finder under your home directory. Go to: Mac HD -> users -> username.

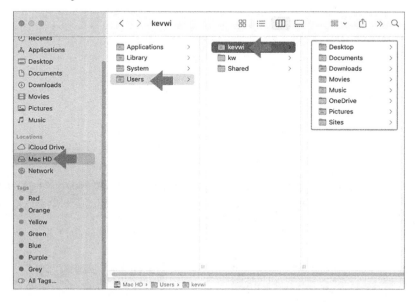

You can move these files to the directories you want them in, eg pictures in the pictures folder, or music in the music folder and so on.

Transfer Files from an old Mac

First, you'll need to make sure both your Macs are on the same network, or the same WiFi.

On your old Mac, open the Migration Assistant. You'll find it in the utilities folder in your finder applications. Click 'continue' and follow the prompts.

When you get to the transfer screen, select 'to another Mac'. Click 'continue'.

On your new Mac, open the Migration Assistant. Click 'continue' and follow the prompts.

When you get to the transfer screen, select 'from a Mac', click 'continue'. Select your old mac from the options. Click 'continue'.

Select the files you want to transfer then click 'continue'.

When transfer finishes on our new Mac, the login window will reappear. Log into the account and follow the prompts.

Getting Around Your Mac

Big Sur's user interface has had a complete makeover. There are new icons on the dock, windows now have a curved edge design and have been freshened up.

In this section, we'll take a look around MacOS Big Sur. We'll explore the desktop, dock, launchpad, stacks and many of the other features on offer.

We'll also take a look at finder, working with files and iCloud.

To help you better understand this section, take a look at the video resources. Open your web browser and navigate to the following sites:

`videos.tips/using-sur`

and

`videos.tips/sur-nav`

The Desktop

The desktop is the main work area on your mac. It's the equivalent of your workbench or office desk, hence why it is called a desktop.

Let's take a look at the different parts of the desktop.

On the top left of your desktop, you'll find the apple menu. From here, you can shut down or restart your mac, open preferences, the app store, lock your screen, and log out.

Along the top of your desktop you'll find the menu bar. On the left hand side you'll find your application menu, and on the right you'll find your status bar.

On your desktop you may find icons for a disk drive or any file you have saved to the desktop. This will depend on how you use your mac.

Along the bottom of your desktop you'll find the dock. Here you'll find your apps, you can also pin apps to the dock. You can resize the dock to suite your needs - make it smaller to give you more space, or make it bigger if you can't see the icons clearly.

The Menu Bar

You'll find the menu bar along the top of your screen, and will look like this:

One thing to notice about the menu bar is it changes according to which application you have showing on your screen. For example, the finder app will have its own menu, iMovie will have a different menu. Keep your eye on the top left hand side of the menu bar as it will have the name of the application currently running in bold type.

Application Menu

The left hand side of the menu bar contains the menu for the app you're currently using. In this example I'm running Safari.

The name of the app appears in bold next to the Apple menu. There are several other app menus, often with standard names such as File, Edit, Format, Window, and Help. Many of the commands in these menus are standard in all apps. For example, the 'open' command is usually in the 'file menu' and the 'copy' command is usually in the 'edit menu'.

Some apps have extra menus with more specific commands native to that app.

Status Menu

The right hand side of the menu bar contains the status menu.

This menu gives feedback on the status of your computer and gives you quick access to certain features - for example; you can quickly turn on Wi-Fi, do a spotlight search, change the audio volume, see date & time, access control center and you can also check messages in notification centre.

If your menu bar is starting to get a bit crowded, you can remove items. To do this, hold down the command key and drag the icon off the menu.

The Dock

The dock has short cuts to applications, such as Music or Photos App. If the app you are looking for isn't here, it will be in the applications folder in finder or on Launchpad.

The apps along the left hand side of the dock represent apps installed on your system. You'll see the finder, siri, and launchpad, along with a few others. On the right hand side you'll see a divider and three apps - these are your most recently used apps and they change according to the apps you use on your Mac.

The next icon on the right is your downloads stack - this is where you'll find the files you've downloaded off the internet.

This folder is called a document stack as it opens out allowing you to see the names of the files without opening the folder, as shown above.

Chapter 3: Getting Around Your Mac

You can also add other folders as stacks to the right hand side of the dock. I'm going to drag my 'documents' folder from the finder window, and drop it next to the 'downloads' icon on the far right of the dock. This creates a stack.

You can also add an app you use a lot to the dock. For example let's add the Chess App to the dock. Open finder, select 'applications' from the panel on the left, then drag the app's icon to the dock.

I'm going to place it between the Maps App and the Contacts App. The icons on the dock will part to allow you do drop the app.

You can also re-order apps on the dock. To do this, click and drag the app to a new position on the dock.

Stacks

You can organise cluttered files on your desktop by automatically stacking them into groups based on the file type - so images are stacked in one pile, documents in another, and so on. To activate desktop stacks, right click on the desktop and select 'use stacks' from the popup menu.

The documents will be stacked neatly on the right hand side of the screen. To open any of the stacks, just click on the icon.

You can also group your stacks by file type (kind), date, or tags. To do this, right click on the desktop and go to 'group stacks by'. From the slide out menu, select an option and see what happens

Launchpad

Launchpad lets you see, organize, and easily open apps installed on your machine. The icons are organized into pages. To access Launchpad, click the icon on your dock, shown below. You can also press F4.

To launch any application, just click on the corresponding icon.

You can organize your applications into folders in Launchpad. Just drag and drop one icon on top of another. For example, you can drag all your reference apps together such as dictionary and calculator into a folder.

Give the folder a name if required. Click the name and type a new one.

When you need to find them you just click on the folder when you open launchpad.

You can also search for apps using the search field at the top of the screen.

Select the app from the results.

If you have a lot of apps installed, you will have multiple pages of apps. Click the page indicators at the bottom of the screen to move between pages.

You can also swipe two fingers across your macbook trackpad.

Spaces & Mission Control

If you use a lot of apps at the same time, your desktop can get a little cluttered. Mac OS has a feature called spaces, that allows you to organize apps onto different virtual desktops called spaces. It's like having more than one desk in your office - different projects will be laid out on different desks. Back on your mac, you can have a desktop that has your email and web browser open, another desktop you could be working on a presentation in Keynote and an accompanying report in Pages App. Another desktop could have photos open and so on.

To open mission control, press F3 on your keyboard. To create new virtual desktop, click the '+' icon on the top right of the screen.

Open the apps you are going to work on. Eg safari web browsing and email.

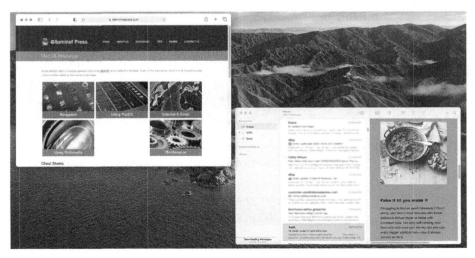

Press F3 again. Click the '+' sign at the top right of the mission control screen to create another virtual desktop. Click the desktop thumbnail that appears on the top bar to switch to that desktop.

On this desktop I'm going to work on my 'international modern architecture' project. For this project, I need Pages and Keynote. So I'd open these apps.

To shift between spaces swipe using 3 fingers on the trackpad on your MacBook. Or press F3 on your keyboard and click the desktop icon at the top of the screen to switch to it.

Now when you want to do some web browsing or check your email, you can go to desktop 1, to carry on with your project go to desktop 2.

103

Finder

This is where all your documents, letters, photographs and favourite music are stored. The finder is like your filing cabinet.

You'll find the finder icon on the far left hand side of your dock.

The finder window is divided into three main parts.

The toolbar across the top of the window contains icons you can customise the way files are displayed. The sidebar which you can use to choose locations and devices on your computer. The main contents, the large pane where all the files and folders are displayed.

Lets take a closer look at the different parts of the finder window.

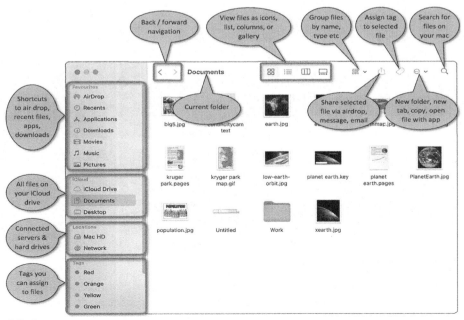

File View Style

The four icons at the top of the finder window allow you to display your file icons in different formats. You can display them as icon view, list view, column view, and gallery view.

Lets take a look at each view...

Icon View. To enter icon view, click the first icon on the top of the window as shown below. This view is useful for scanning through photographs or videos.

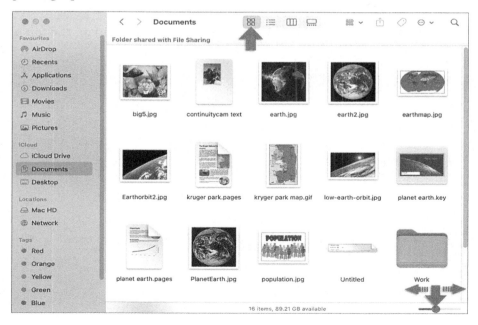

The slider on the status bar along the bottom of the window will resize the icons and previews. If you don't see the status bar, go to the view menu and select 'show status bar'.

Chapter 3: Getting Around Your Mac

List View. To enter list view, select the second icon on the top of the screen, as shown below.

This is useful for looking through documents and file names. You can sort the list according to name, size date, or type - just click on the column headers.

Column View. To enter column view, select the third icon on the top of the screen, as shown below.

This is useful if you are looking through files that are stored in lots of folders, as you can open up the folders in each column and view the contents side by side.

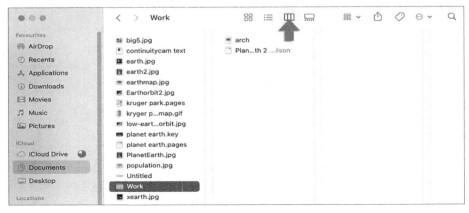

Gallery View. To enter gallery view, select the fourth icon on the top of the screen, as shown below.

This is useful for scanning through photographs, videos, documents, or music. Thumbnail previews of the files appear in the bottom third of the window with a larger preview of the selected file in the top half of the window.

On the right hand side you'll see some details about the file such as date created, date modified, resolution and tags. This is the preview pane.

To hide or show preview pane, go to the view menu, then select 'show preview' or 'hide preview'.

Markup

Markup allows you to annotate documents and photographs just by opening up a preview, rather than opening the file in an app.

In finder, select the folder the image or document is saved in. Right click on the icon. From the popup menu go down to 'quick actions', select 'markup' from the slideout.

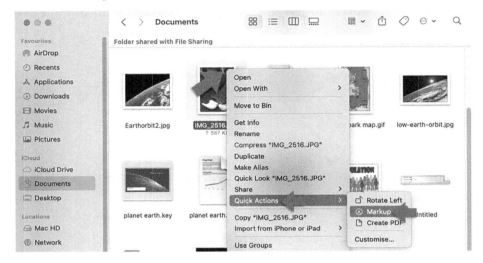

Once the markup screen appears, you can add text, shapes and colour.

I'm going to add a shape. Click the small down arrow next to the shape icon and select a shape.

Draw the shape on the image, and double click inside it to add some text.

To change the size, colour and font, click the small down arrow next to the font icon on the toolbar. From the drop down menu, you can select a font, change the colour and size, change the typeface to bold italic or underlined, and also change the text alignment.

Click 'done' on the top right of the toolbar when you're finished, or click the 'share' icon to send your file with the annotations to someone else.

Markup using your iPad

You can also send documents and images to your iPad for annotation. To do this, select the finder app on your dock.

Select the folder where the document is saved. Right click on the document, go down to 'quick actions', then select 'markup' from the slideout.

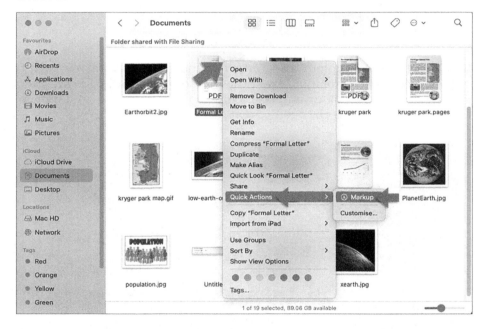

You can use the markup feature on images such as jpeg, or png, and PDF documents.

You'll also find the markup tools in the preview screen. Select document, then press space bar.

Now on your iPad, you'll see the markup screen appear. *If it doesn't appear automatically, click the 'markup on iPad' icon on the top of the toolbar on the markup window on your Mac.*

On your iPad, use your finger or the pencil to annotate your document. You'll see a live update on your Mac as you do so.

On your iPad you can select different pens, highlighters from the toolbar along the bottom of the screen, as well as change the size and opacity.

Tap 'done' on the top right of your iPad screen when you're finished.

Click 'done' on the top right of the markup window on your Mac to save the annotations.

Tags

Tags allow you to place markers onto your documents so you can find them more easily. First, rename the tags to something more meaningful. To do this, open finder, click on the finder menu on the top left, then select 'preferences'

Click on the 'tags' tab at the top of the preferences window.

You will see a list of the colour tags, and a few more at the bottom such as, 'Work', 'Home', and 'Important'.

To change the colour of a tag, click on the little bubble and choose a colour.

To change the name of the tag, click on the tag title, and type your new tag name.

To create a new tag, click the '+' icon on the bottom left and enter a name.

Enter a name for your tag, eg 'work'.

Assign a colour.

Add the tag to the shortcut menu. To do this drag the tag over the tag you want to replace in the favourites section at the bottom of the window.

The favourites section shows up on the left had pane in finger under 'tags', and in the shortcut menu.

Tagging Files

To tag a file, click the document you want to tag then select the tags icon. From the list, select the tag that describes the category of your document, eg work.

You can also use a keyboard shortcut to tag files quickly. Select the file, then press Control 1 - 7 to add the tag. Control - 0 clears tags.

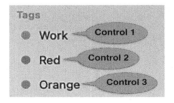

The control keys relate to the order in the 'tags' list on the left hand side.

Smart Folders

Smart folders can be quite useful for keeping track of files. Smart folders allow you to create search parameters and save them as a folder. So for example, you could create a folder that displays the files you worked on in the last 30 days, or show all your photos, documents, and so on.

First, open finder. Select a location to search, eg iCloud Drive.

To create a smart folder, open your finder app and click the 'file' menu. From the menu select 'new smart folder'.

Along the top of the smart folder window, select where you want to search for files. We're searching iCloud Drive so click 'iCloud Drive'.

If you want to search your whole mac, select 'this mac'.

Now we need to create the search criteria for our smart folder. Click the '+' icon on the right.

In this example, I want to show all the documents I've worked on in the last 30 days. Click the 'any' field and select 'document'.

You'll see a list of documents appear in the window. Now we need to add another criteria. We wanted a smart folder to show all documents we worked on in the last 30 days. So, click the '+' icon on the right.

Select the 'last opened date' and from the drop down select 'last modified'. In the next field set it to 'within last'. In the next field enter the number of days: 30. In the last field, set it to 'days'.

Click 'save' on the top right.

Give your smart folder a meaningful name in the 'save as' field. Save it in 'saved searches', and make sure 'add to sidebar' is ticked. Click 'save'.

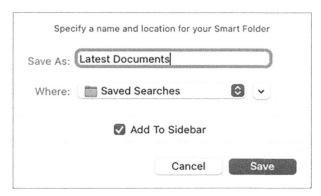

Your smart folder will appear on your finder's sidebar.

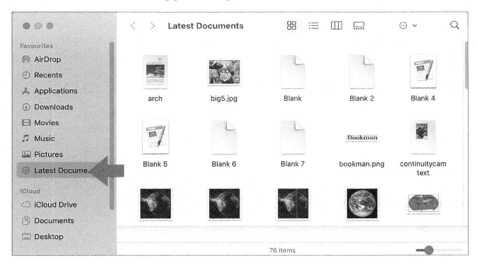

Try creating smart folders with some other criteria using the same procedure as above.

Quick Preview Files

When browsing through your files in finder, you can preview the file without opening it. This works well with photos, documents and videos.

To preview a file, click the file to select it, then press the space bar on your keyboard. A window will popup displaying a preview version of the file.

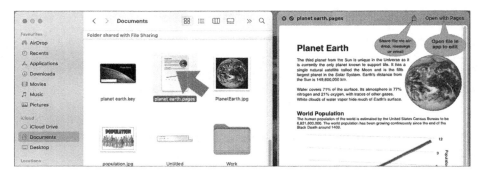

On the toolbar along the top, you can open the file in the appropriate app to edit it, or you can share the file via email or social media.

Compress Files

You can compress files into zip archives right within finder. These can be useful if you intend to send a lot of files over email, messaging or if you're making multiple files available for download.

To compress files, select them in finder - hold down the CMD key to select multiple files. Then right click on the selection, from the popup menu select 'compress items'.

You'll see a new file appear called **archive.zip**. This is the file that will contain all the files you selected. You can rename and send this file.

Accessing External Drives

When you plug in a USB flash drive or an external hard drive like the one below, an icon will appear on your desktop.

Double click this icon to open the drive in finder.

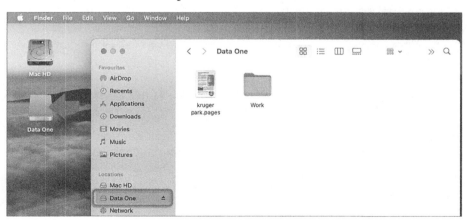

Note before unplugging the drive, it is good practice to eject the drive by clicking on the eject icon next to the drive name in finder.

Accessing Data CDs and DVDs

Macs no longer include DVD or CD drives. If you want to listen to a CD, watch a DVD or access files on disc, you'll need to buy an external USB DVD drive.

Plug the DVD drive into a spare USB port and insert your disc. An icon will appear on your desktop. Double click on the icon to open the disc contents in finder.

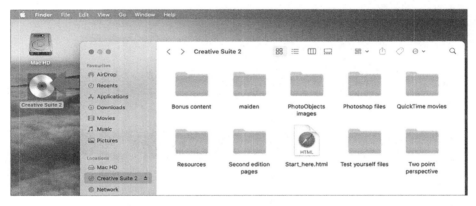

Notice the DVD/CD drive is selected under 'devices' on the left hand panel of the finder window.

In the main finder window, you'll see all the files and folders contained on the disc. Double click on any of these to open them up.

To eject your disc. Click the eject icon next to the DVD/CD drive on the left hand panel in finder.

Sharing Files on a Network

You can share files across your home network. This is useful if you are sharing resources such as documents with other people who are connected to your network and is ideal for transferring larger files.

To set up file sharing, open your system preferences and double click 'sharing'.

On the left hand side turn on file sharing.

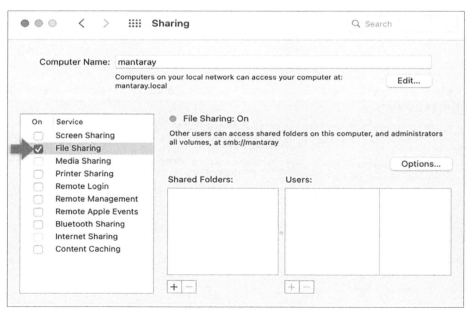

Remember the 'computer name'. In this example it's 'mantaray'. You'll need it when connecting to this machine later on.

Now, select the folder you want to share. Under 'shared folders', click the plus sign and select a folder on your mac you want to share.

Select the folder you want to share. Click 'add'.

Select the users to whom you want to grant access. Under 'users' click the plus sign.

Select the name of the person you want to give access to your folder

Next select what access you want to give them: read only or read & write. Click the selector next to the name to change this. If you want anyone to be able to access the folder, set 'everyone' to 'read & write' or 'read only'.

If you are going to connect to this folder from a windows or linux machine, you'll need to enable SMB support. To do this, click options.

Connect to a Shared Folder on Another Computer

You can connect to shared resources on a network or the internet. You can connect to another computer running Windows 10, Windows Server, Linux or MacOS. To start, open finder from the dock then click the 'go' menu at the top of the screen, select 'connect to server'.

To connect to a shared folder located on a linux or windows computer, you'll need to use the SMB protocol.

For example...

```
smb://orion/public
```

Where 'orion' is the server or computer name and 'public' is the shared folder on that server or computer. Click the plus sign on the left hand side to add the server address you just entered to the 'favorite server' list. Click 'connect' to connect. You may be prompted for a username and password - this will be the username that you use to log into the server or computer you're trying to connect to, and will probably be different from the username and password you used to log onto your mac.

You can also connect to FTP servers using the same method, except use ftp:// instead followed by your FTP username, then server name.

```
ftp://kevwils@ftp.myftpserver.com
```

You'll be prompted for your username and password for that server. You can usually obtain this from your internet service provider.

124

Finder Preferences

You can customise finder to your own needs. To do this, in finder, click the 'finder' menu and select 'preferences'

Along the top of the window you'll see four tabs. From the 'general' tab you can select which icons to show on the desktop - your external hard disks, flash drives, and your internal hard disk, as well as any CD/DVDs and server shared folders you're connected to. You can also select which folder appears automatically when you open finder.

Under the 'tags' tab, you can customise your tags. See "Tags" on page 112 for more information.

Under the 'sidebar' tab, you can customise the shortcuts you see listed down the left hand side of your finger window. Click the check boxes next to the shortcuts you want to add, remove the tickbox next to the shortcuts you want to remove.

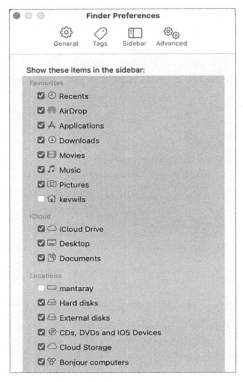

From the 'advanced' tab, you can show/hide filename extensions, set finder warnings, keep folders on top of other windows, and the default search location when using finder search.

iCloud Drive

iCloud Drive is Apple's cloud storage service for devices running iOS, iPadOS, MacOS, and Windows 10. This feature allows users to save photos, videos, Keynote, Pages, Numbers files, and music to the cloud.

Using iCloud Drive

Once you have signed in with your Apple ID on your Mac, you will find iCloud Drive on the side panel in your finder app.

To start using iCloud drive, you can save documents from any of your Applications. For example, say you are working on a document in Pages, you can save it in the 'documents' section of iCloud drive as shown below.

Chapter 3: Getting Around Your Mac

Now if I want to carry on with my document I can get my 'documents' folder on my iPad/iPhone. Select 'icloud drive' from the panel on the left, then tap 'documents'.

The document was saved in the 'documents' folder. If you tap in the 'documents' folder you will find your saved document.

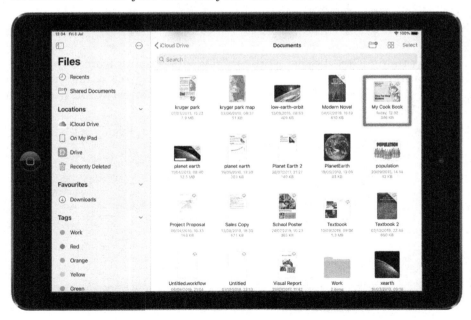

Tap on the file icon to open it up. Note, you'll need the same app on your iPad as you used on your Mac to edit the documents. In this example, I used Pages word processor installed on Mac and iPad. You can download the apps from the app store if you need them.

iCloud Drive File Sharing

Any file in iCloud Drive can now be shared with another person through a new link feature. The link option will give direct access to specific files and folders while keeping the rest of your iCloud Drive private.

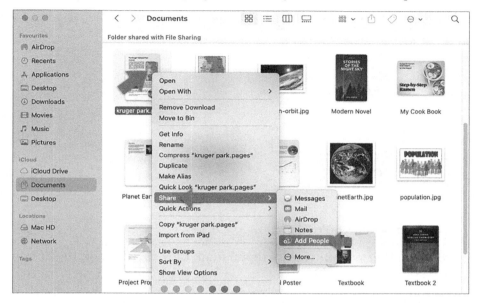

Select how you want to share the link with the other person. In this example I'm going to send it via email. Click 'add people', to grant permission to a person to view your file.

Click 'mail' to share by email, then adjust the options below. Set 'who can access' to anyone with a link. If you just want the person you're sharing with to see the file, leave this setting on its default.

Enter the person's email address in the 'to' field, add a subject if you wish. In the message body, you'll see an icon representing the shared file. Just above the icon, type a message.

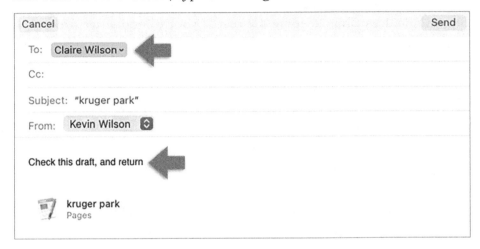

Click 'send' when you're done.

When the other person checks their email, they can click on the link in the email to see your file.

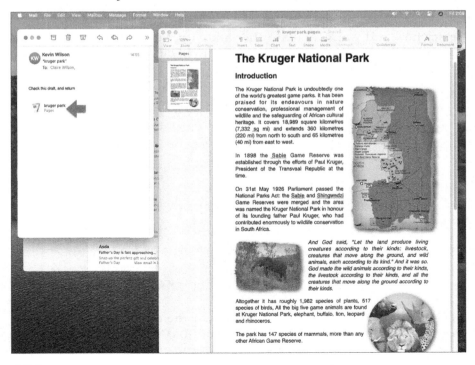

If the other person is on a Windows machine, they can click the link to download.

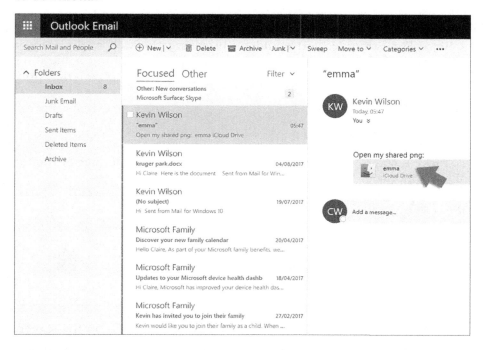

Click 'download a copy' from the prompt.

Managing App Windows

When working on your Mac it's best to arrange the windows on your desktop, especially when you're using more than one application at a time. For example, you could be browsing the web and writing a document at the same time- perhaps you're researching something, you could have the Pages App open and your web browser next to it on the screen.

Moving a Window

To move a window, move your mouse pointer to the title bar at the top of the window.

Now click and drag the window to your desired position on the screen.

Release your mouse button. You can move the windows to anywhere on the desktop.

Resizing a Window

To resize a window, move your mouse pointer to the bottom right corner of the window - your pointer should turn into a double edged arrow.

The double edged arrow means you can resize the window. Now click and drag the edge of the window until it is the size you want.

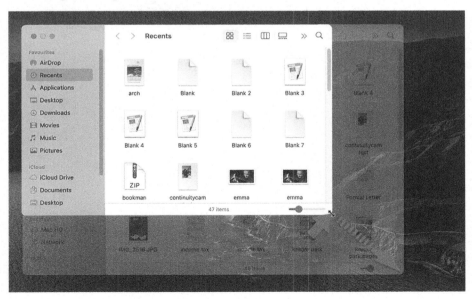

You can drag any edge of the window - left, bottom or right edge, but I find using the corner allows you to freely resize the window much more easily.

Minimise, Maximise & Close a Window

On the top left hand side of every window, you'll see three little icons. These three icons appear on all apps that run in a window.

Lets take a closer look at an example. Here's the finder window.

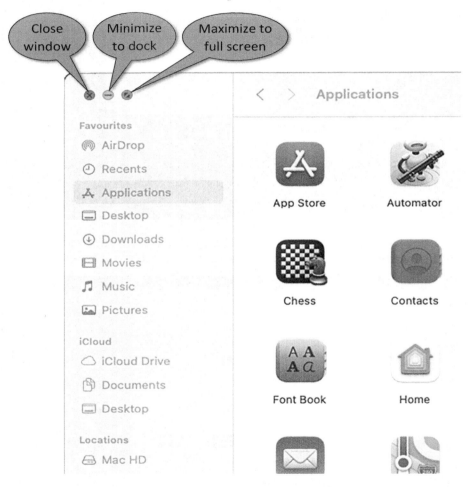

Use the first icon to close the window. Note that this doesn't close the app fully.

The second icon will minimise the window to the space on the right hand side of the dock.

The third icon will maximise the window so it fills the entire screen, or if the window is already maximised, using the same icon, restore the window to its original size.

Spotlight Search

Spotlight is a search engine that allows you to locate anything on your Mac, iCloud or the web.

If you look in the top right hand corner of the screen, you'll see what looks like a magnifying glass. Click the icon and type in what you're searching for.

You'll see a list of top hits which are the closest matches to your search query and a list of suggestions.

Spotlight can also give you definitions of words, convert currencies, temperatures, measurements, and make calculations.

To customise the search parameters, open system preferences then double click 'spotlight'. Select 'search results'. Select the apps, categories and file types you want to appear in the search results.

Select 'privacy', click the + icon on the bottom left, then select folders you want to exclude from the search results.

Notification Centre

Notification Centre is a side panel that shows alerts from apps such as new email, new messages, reminders, calendar events and system alerts. As well as an assortment of widgets.

To open notification centre, click the clock on the top right.

Notification Centre has been redesigned and now puts all notifications and widgets together on a single page. You'll see alerts from applications at the top.

Underneath, you'll see new widgets for local weather, calendar and reminders

Notifications

At the top of notification centre you'll see your alerts and messages, such as new email, new tweets, new events, current song etc.

There are three types of notifications: banners, alerts, and badges.

Banners

These are displayed for a short period in the upper right corner of the screen for a few seconds, then slide off to the right. Click banner to open app.

The application's icon is displayed on the left side of the banner, while the message from the application will be displayed on the right side.

Alerts

Same as banners, except an alert has a call to action on the right hand side and will not disappear from the screen until the user takes action. Click the action button on the bottom right of the alert to open the app.

Badges

These are red notification icons that are displayed on the application's icon. They indicate the number of items available for the application.

Notification Settings

Open the system preferences. Select the apple menu on the top left, then click 'system preferences'.

From the system preferences window, double click 'notifications'.

This allows you to set how the alerts and notifications appear on your screen when events happen. Select an app from the list on the left.

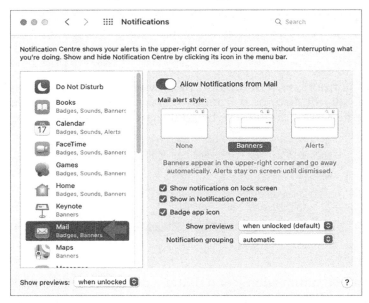

This will show you the notification settings for that app. You can allow/ disallow notifications for the selected app, or you can change the alert style (banners and alerts).

You can choose whether to show the app's notifications on the lock screen, notification center, or show the notification badge on the app's icon.

138

Widgets

You can add more widgets by clicking 'edit widgets' at the bottom of the screen.

Scroll down the list. For example, I'm going to add the world clock widget. Select the size of widget you want to add - small, medium, and on some widgets, large.

Drag and drop the widget onto the notification centre on the right.

Click 'done' when you're finished.

Control Centre

A new control centre introduced in MacOS Big Sur, allows you to control common settings such as Wi-Fi, Bluetooth, AirDrop, music, volume control and screen brightness without having to go into the settings app.

To open control centre, click the control icon on the top right of your screen.

Here, you can control your display brightness, volume, as well as wifi, bluetooth and airdrop. Just click on the icons to adjust.

You can drag and pin your most used items from control centre to the top of your menu bar for easy one-click access.

Add controls for the apps and features you use most, such as fast user switching, battery status and accessibility features.

Open the system preferences. Select the apple menu on the top left, then click 'system preferences'.

From the system preferences window, double click 'dock and menu bar'.

From the list on the left hand side of the settings window, select a shortcut to add to control centre.

Click the tick box next to 'show in control centre'

Handoff

Handoff is a continuity feature that allows you to start something on one device such as your iPhone or iPad, then seamlessly pick up and continue on another such as your Mac.

First, you'll need to enable Handoff on your devices. To enable Handoff on your iPhone, open the settings app from your home screen. Tap 'General', then 'Handoff'. Tap the switch to set 'Handoff' to 'on'.

Now enable your Bluetooth. Go to the settings app, select 'Bluetooth'. Tap the switch to set it to 'on'.

To enable it on your Mac, go to the System Preferences in the Apple menu. Tap 'Bluetooth' and turn it on.

Go back to System Preferences and click 'General'. Click the check box next to "Allow Handoff between this Mac and your iCloud Devices".

Now for this demo, I'm going to start typing an email message on my iPhone. When you bring your iPhone near your Mac, you'll see the icon of the app you're using, appear on the right hand side of the dock.

Click on this icon on the dock to continue using the app. In this demo, you'll see the email open up on your Mac.

Here, you'll be able to continue from where you left off.

SideCar

Sidecar allows you to use your iPad as a second screen on a Mac running MacOS Big Sur. For Sidecar to work, both your Mac and iPad must be signed in with the same iCloud account. Both devices must also be connected using a USB cable or Bluetooth. Sidecar works with the latest Apple hardware, so some older iPads and Macs wont work. You'll need a Mac that is 'Late 2015 or newer'.

First, set up Sidecar on your Mac. To do this, click the system preferences, then select 'Sidecar'.

Click the 'connect to' drop down menu.

Select your iPad from the dropdown menu.

Your iPad will connect to your mac.

Once your iPad connects to your Mac, you'll see an extended desktop on your iPad.

Let's take a look at Sidecar's interface on the iPad... Along the left hand side of the screen you'll see a toolbar.

Chapter 3: Getting Around Your Mac

You can quickly send apps to your iPad screen. To do this, click and hold your mouse pointer on the green expansion button on the left top of an app. From the drop down menu select 'move to iPad'.

If you use any graphic apps such as illustrator or photoshop, Sidecar allows you to use your iPad as a graphics tablet.

Load up your graphics program on your Mac, then send it over to your iPad using the feature above.

Now, with your pencil, you can draw directly onto the screen.

You can arrange your displays. On your Mac, open the settings app, select display, then select the 'arrangement' tab.

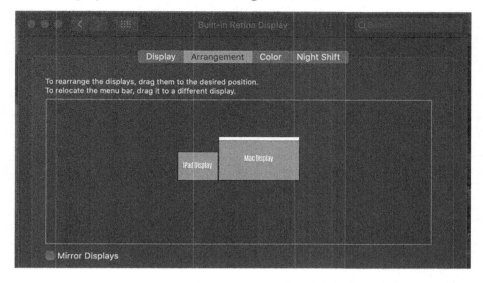

Your main laptop or mac display is represented by the large blue rectangle. Your iPad display is represented by the small blue rectangle.

If you use your iPad on the left hand side of your mac, move the small blue rectangle to the left of the large blue rectangle. If you use your iPad on the right hand side, move the small blue rectangle to the right. This makes it easier when dragging windows from your Mac to your iPad, so you drag them to the side of the Mac's screen on the same side as where your iPad is.

In the illustration, my iPad is on the left hand side, so I'd move the small blue rectangle to the left of the large blue rectangle. So now whenever I drag an app to my iPad, I drag it to the left where my iPad is physically.

Universal Clipboard

This is another interesting feature that allows you to cut, copy and paste with your clipboard across all your Apple Devices; iPhone, iPad as well as your Mac. This works when all your devices are logged in with your apple id.

In the demonstration below, I have copied a paragraph from a Pages document on the Macbook Pro, and pasted it into an email on my iPhone.

To do this, highlight the text from an application on your Mac, right click and click copy.

On your iPad or iPhone, go into the application you are going to paste the text into, tap and hold your finger in the position you want the text to appear, and tap paste from the menu that appears.

Universal Clipboard also works the other way around, if you wanted to copy some text from your phone and paste into a document on your Mac.

Using Siri

Siri has finally made it to the Mac and works pretty much as she does on the iPhone.

You can find Siri on the top right hand side of your screen. Or hold down command space on your keyboard for two seconds.

Try some of the following phrases...

See what Siri does.

Voice Control

You can give voice commands to your mac. To do this, first you will need to enable the feature. Go to system preferences.

Click 'accessibility'.

Select 'voice control' from the list on the left hand side.

Click the tick box next to 'enable voice control'. When you enable this, a microphone indicator will appear on the screen.

Try saying "open safari", or "scroll to the top". To pause voice control say "go to sleep" or click 'sleep' on the microphone indicator. To resume say or click 'wake up' on the microphone indicator.

To see all the commands you can give, click 'commands' in the voice control preferences.

Voice Dictation

Instead of typing text, you can actually dictate the work using a microphone. Dictation converts your spoken words into text.

First you'll need to enable dictation. To do this, open the system preferences.

Select 'keyboard' from the system preferences window.

Select the 'dictation' tab. Click the check box to enable dictation.

Now, you can use dictation in any app that supports text, such as notes, pages, email, and so on. To begin, position your cursor in your document then tap the 'fn' key twice.

You'll see a mic icon appear next to your document. Now you can begin dictating your notes.

As well as entering text by dictation, you can also add punctuation. To enter a punctuation mark or symbol, just speak its name.

To insert a question mark say "question mark"
To insert a period mark to end a sentence say "period" or "full stop"
To insert a comma, say "comma".

You can also move your cursor to enter text in different parts of your document. Try these...

"Move forward one paragraph" or "move up one line"
"Select next word".
"Select next paragraph."

You can format text. For example, if I wanted to enter a word or sentence in bold text, speak the word or sentence, then immediately after say "bold that". Use "italicalise that", for italic, and "underline that" to underline the text.

To see all the voice commands, open system preferences, select 'accessibility', click 'voice control' on the left hand side, then click 'commands'.

Using Apple Pay on your Mac

To be able to use Apple Pay on your Mac, you will need to use the Safari Web Browser and have an Apple device such as your iPhone near by. On participating websites, you will see "pay with Apple Pay Button". When you click on this button, you will see an authentication prompt on your nearby iPhone or Apple Watch. This uses the continuity feature.

Browse your favourite shopping site and, when you're ready to buy, click on the Apple Pay button.

Once you click the Apple Pay button on the website, a notification will pop up on your iPhone asking you to authorise the transaction. You can do this by using Touch ID or Face ID on your iPhone. If you're using a macbook with a fingerprint scanner, tap the touch sensor to authorise the transaction.

You'll only see the Apple Pay logos on participating websites and only if you have your iPhone set up and in the vicinity of your Mac.

Auto Unlock

You can automatically unlock your Mac using another Apple Device such as Apple Watch.

Open your Macbook's lid or tap a key while wearing your Apple Watch to unlock your Mac from sleep mode.

Auto Unlock only works when waking your Mac from sleep. If you restart your Mac or start it up from Shut Down, then you will need to enter a password to unlock.

First you need to enable 'two factor authentication'. To do this, open your web browser and head over to...

```
appleid.apple.com
```

...and enter your Apple ID and password.

Click 'edit' under the security section, then 'get started' under 'two step verification' and follow the on screen prompts.

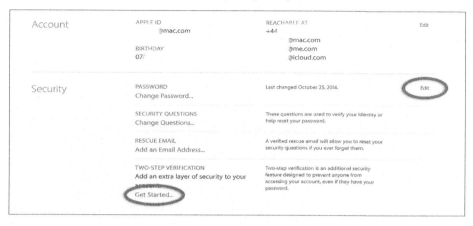

Now, go to system preferences, click 'security & privacy'.

Select the general tab, click 'use your apple watch to unlock apps and your mac'. *Click the lock on the bottom left if all the options are greyed out.*

Enter your mac password.

Once set up, you can wake and unlock your Mac simply by opening up the lid, or tapping a key while wearing your watch.

The Mac Keyboard

The Mac keyboard is not much different from a standard computer keyboard, although there are a few keys to take note of. These are highlighted below.

Macs have a few special keys that allow you to carry out certain operations on your mac.

The Command Key

This is equivalent to the control key on a PC, and allows you to use keyboard shortcuts for various commands available on the menu in different applications. For example, to undo something press Command-Z, to save press Command-S to print press Command-P and so on.

156

The Option Key

Also known as the Alt Key, allows you to select which drive to boot from when your Mac starts. Useful if you need to boot your mac from a start-up disk.

The Control Key

This key allows you to use the right click option on your mouse. Hold down control and click the mouse button.

The Function Key

This key is used to perform special functions with the 'F' keys along the top on a MacBook keyboard.

Executing Keyboard Shortcuts

Hold down one of the keys above, then tap the letter corresponding to the command you want to execute, as shown below.

Useful Keyboard Shortcuts

Use the command key on your keyboard to execute these commands.

Using the command key, you can execute several commands common to most applications

⌘ + P = Print

Q = Quit

X = Qut   W = Close Window

Z = Undo   C = Copy

A = Select All   S = Save

H = Hide   V = Paste

F = Find   O = Open Window

G = Find Next   E = Eject

M = Minimize   N = New

- = Zoom Out   + = Zoom In

If you're having some trouble with an application, you can force it to quit using the combo: command option escape

⌘ + ⌥ + ⎋

Select the application from the popup window and click 'force quit'.

158

MacOS Startup Keys

When your Mac starts up, you can hit certain keys to use different tools. This is particularly useful if your Mac encounters problems or you want to re-install MacOS - eg, hold down option key to select boot device.

When your Mac restarts, quickly hold down the keyboard combo until you see the Apple logo.

Keyboard Combo	Command
Shift ⇧	Start up in safe mode with minimal drivers.
Option ⌥	Open start up manager. Allows you to select boot device.
C	Start up from a bootable CD, DVD, or USB thumb drive
D	Run Apple Hardware Test.
Option D	Run Apple Hardware Test over the Internet.
Option N	Start up from a NetBoot server using an image stored on MacOS Server.
Command R	Start up in Recovery Mode using local recovery partition.
Command Option R	Start up in Recovery Mode using recovery data from Apple's Servers.
Command Option P R	Reset NVRAM. Hold keys until you hear startup sound.
T	Start up in target disk mode, allows your mac to be used as if it was an external hard drive.

Use both the shift, command and option keys to execute these commands.

Command Key   Option Key

Making Gestures

If you have a Macbook with a trackpad, you can use a number of finger gestures to operate certain features of MacOS.

One Finger Point and Tap

You can move your mouse pointer across the screen by using one finger on the trackpad. Tap your finger on the pad to select an icon and is the equivalent of your left mouse click.

Right Click

Tap with two fingers on the trackpad. You can also hold down the control key and tap with one finger.

Two Finger Scroll

You can scroll down web pages and documents using two fingers on the track pad.

Two Finger Rotate

You can rotate things on the screen by using your forefinger and thumb on the trackpad making a twisting action with your wrist. This works well when viewing photographs or browsing a map.

Two Finger Swipe

Swiping two fingers across the trackpad swipes between pages in a document, book or on a website.

Four Finger Open Launchpad

Use your thumb and three fingers on the trackpad and draw your fingers and thumb together will open Launchpad where you can select an app to open.

162

Magic Mouse

A Bluetooth wireless mouse with multi gesture support. We'll take a look at these gestures below.

Left Click

Primary select button to click or double click on an icon

Right Click

Secondary click or right mouse button click to reveal context menus. Click with two fingers on your mouse. You can also hold down the control key and click your mouse button.

Scrolling

Scroll vertically or horizontally around a page, image, document, etc.
Hold your mouse still then run your finger over the surface of the
mouse - up and down, left and right to scroll pages

Swipe

Hold your mouse still, then use two fingers to swipe left and right
across the surface of the mouse to move a page forward or backward
when reading a document or website.

Find your Mouse Pointer

If you have lost your mouse pointer somewhere on the screen you can wiggle your finger backwards and forwards across your track-pad .

Wiggle your mouse and your cursor will grow to a larger size making it easier to find.

The Touch Bar

On the newer Macbooks, you'll find another navigation bar along the top of your keyboard. This is called the Touch Bar.

Touch Bar Layout

On the Touch Bar, you can tap icons and swipe through lists to aid your navigation on screen.

Icons on the 'application strip' of the Touch Bar change depending on the app you're using. For example, if you're using the photo app, you'll find icons to crop or rotate an image or scroll through your photos. For the mail app, you'll find icons for replying to or deleting emails. In maps app, you'll find icons to rotate or zoom into a map.

The Touch Bar is broken down into the following general layout.

Control Strip

Click on the desktop and you'll see these icons on the touch bar. On the right hand side, you'll see the control strip. Tap the left arrow to expand the strip to reveal all the icons.

Once you expand the bar to show all the icons. This is where you'll find your icons to increase/decrease screen brightness, desktop spaces, launchpad, increase/decrease keyboard illumination brightness, skip previous track, play pause, skip next track, mute volume, decrease/ increase volume, and ask siri.

Tap the x on the left hand side to close the control strip.

Application Strip

The application strip is the middle section of the touch bar where you can control common actions in various Mac Apps such as Safari, Mail, Photos and so on. So for example, if you open Safari web browser, the application strip will look like this.

You'll see icons for all your most recently visited websites. Swipe left and right over the Touch Bar to see all the icons. Tap on an icon to open the corresponding website.

Once you've navigated to a website, the Touch Bar icons will change again.

Tap on 'search or enter website name' to do a Google Search or enter a website address in Safari, then type into the search field on the screen.

You can also use the Touch Bar with other Apps. For example if you open the Mail App the Touch Bar shows your common task toolbar.

If you compose or reply to a message, the Touch Bar changes to show your formatting tools. Tap on any of the icons with your finger.

Try the Photos App, when you open the app, the Touch Bar shows.

You can slide your finger across the thumbnail navigation on the center of the Touch Bar to scroll through your photos.

You'll find that the Touch Bar will change according to the app that is currently running. Note that not all apps support this feature.

Customise Touch Bar

You can tweak the Touch Bar to your own preferences. To do this, open the app you want to customise, eg Finder. From the drop down menu, select 'Customise Touch Bar'.

Now from the touch icon selections on your screen, click and drag the icon you want to the touch bar.

You can also tap and drag the icons to reorder them or move them.

To remove an icon, drag it off the Touch Bar.

Click 'done' on the top left of the icon selection pane when you're finished.

Taking Screenshots

You can capture a screenshot of the entire screen, or just a portion of it. You can either save the screenshot as a file on the desktop or to the clipboard, where you can paste into another app.

Command-Shift-3 captures the whole screen and saves it as a PNG file on the desktop.

Command-Control-Shift-3 captures the whole screen and saves to your clipboard.

Command-Shift-4 captures a selected portion of the screen and saves it as a PNG file on the desktop.

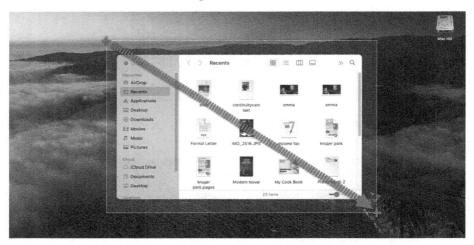

Command-Control-Shift-4 captures a selected portion of the screen and saves it to your clipboard.

Command-Shift-5 opens up the on-screen capture controls.

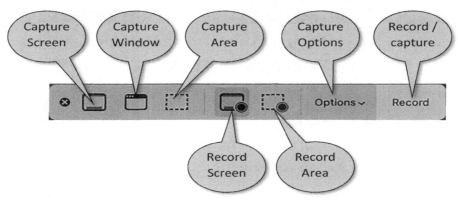

Select 'capture screen' to capture the full screen, select 'capture window' then click the window you want to capture, select 'capture area' then click and drag the box around the area of the screen you want. Click 'capture'. Your screenshot or recording will appear on your desktop.

Screen Recording

Press **Command-Shift-5**. Click 'record screen' icon. Click 'options' to change save location, timer, microphone or show/hide mouse pointer etc.

Click the stop icon on the top right of your screen to stop recording.

Your recording will appear as an MP4 video file on your desktop.

Split Screen Mode

You can arrange your windows side by side. Open the two apps you want to arrange side by side, eg: Pages & Safari. Left click and hold your mouse button down on the app's green maximize button on the top-left hand side.

Select 'tile window to left of screen'.

Select the other window to arrange them side by side...

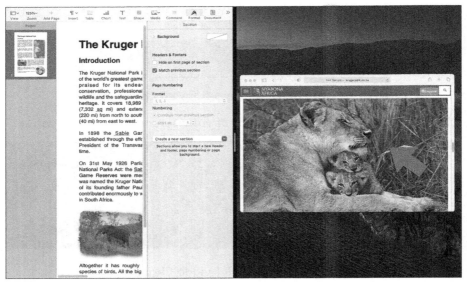

Split Screen opens in full screen mode, so you wont see the Dock or Menu Bar.

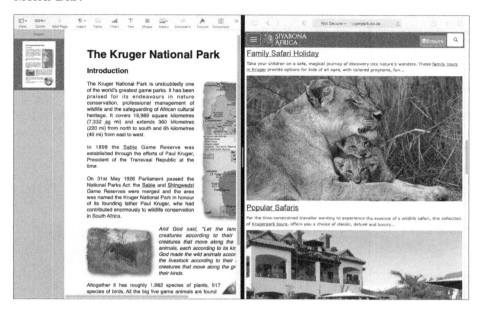

Move your mouse pointer to the top edge of the screen to reveal the Menu Bar.

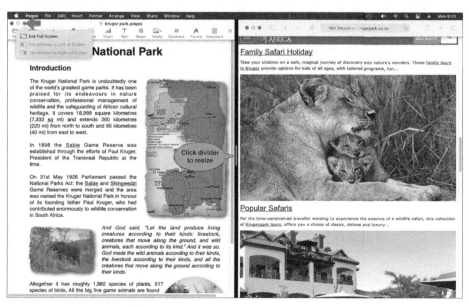

Click the green maximise button again to return to desktop view. Do this with both apps to return them to normal mode.

Digitally Sign a Document

MacOS includes a signature creation feature in the preview app. You can import an image of your handwritten signature and use it to sign any documents you need to.

First, sign your name on a blank sheet of white paper using a black marker.

Hit launch pad and open the preview app, click the 'tools' menu, go down to 'annotate', then 'signature. From the slideout select 'manage signatures'.

Select 'camera'.

Now hold the signature you wrote down on your sheet of paper up to the camera.

Make sure your signature fills the whole window on the screen. Click 'done'.

Now open the PDF document you want to sign, click the markup icon on the top right of the toolbar and select 'the signature icon.

Click your signature. You might need to drag your signature into place.

175

Keychain

Keychain is your password manager. Keychain allows you to save passwords so you don't have to remember them when you access an account on a website, or when you check your email, or connect to a network server. When you sign into these services for the first time you'll be given the option to save the password.

Or in MacOS, you can select the option to save your password.

You'll find all your saved passwords on your keychain app. To open the app, select 'launchpad' from the dock.

Select 'other'.

176

Click 'keychain access' to start the app.

Lets take a look at the keychain app. Along the top of the app window you can add a new password, or change, view and update password information.

On the 'keychains' pane along the left hand side, you'll see some keychains. Here, under 'logon' you'll see sites or services for which have saved passwords for - this could be a server on a network, a website such as facebook, or the mail app. Under 'icloud' you'll see sites or services whose passwords have synced from other devices such as an iPhone or iPad. Under 'system' you'll see wifi networks that you've saved passwords for.

On the middle pane you'll see a list of sites/services for which you have passwords saved for on the keychain that is selected in the left hand 'keychains' panel. You can double click on a service in the list to view, change password or account username.

Using Applications

MacOS comes with a lot of apps pre-installed. You'll find an app for storing photos, listening to music, watching movies or tv programmes. You'll find an app for catching up on the news, reading books, taking notes, surfing the web and email, as well as productivity apps such as word processors, spreadsheets, video editing and so on.

You can also download countless apps from the app store.

In this chapter we'll take a look at the various apps installed on your Mac

To help you better understand this section, take a look at the video resources. Open your web browser and navigate to the following sites:

videos.tips/using-sur

Launching Your Applications

You can find applications on the dock at the bottom of your screen.

You can also find apps by hitting the Launch Pad icon on the dock.

If there are apps you use a lot, you can drag them from launch pad to the dock.

The next time you need the application just click on the icon on the dock.

Chapter 4: Using Applications

You can also launch applications from the 'applications' folder in your finder window. Click the finder icon on the dock, then click the 'applications' folder.

If the application you launched is one you use quite often, but is not permanently on the dock, you can easily add it. To do this, right click on the icon, go to options, and from the slideout click 'keep in dock'.

This will keep the application's icon in the dock whether it is running or not.

Killing Unresponsive Apps

Sometimes apps lock up and freeze and there is no way to close the app using conventional means.

Press **CMD - OPTION - ESC**, as shown below...

From the popup window, select the app you want to shut down, then click 'force quit'.

App Store

The App Store allows you to browse and download apps developed for your Mac. You'll find the icon on your launchpad or dock.

You can also access the app store from the apple menu on the very top left of the screen.

Once you launch app store, you'll see the main screen. Here you can type in the name of the app you are looking for in the search field on the top left of the screen, or click the 'categories' icon to browse categories such as reference, productivity and entertainment listed down the panel on the left hand side.

182

To buy or download anything, just click the price - or click 'get' if it's free.

The buttons will change to 'buy app', or 'install' if it's free. Click on the icon again to confirm the download.

Sign in with your Apple ID email and password if prompted.

The app will download. Once the install is complete, you will find your new app in Launchpad or in the applications folder in Finder.

App Tabs

The tabs feature allows you to open multiple application windows as tabs in the same window.

You can merge all your open windows using the 'merge all windows' command. To do this click the 'window' menu at the top of your screen. Select 'merge all windows'.

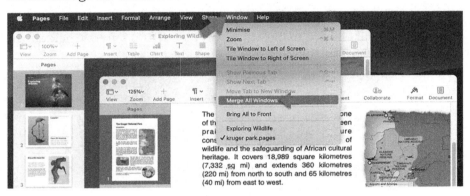

This will merge all the open windows of the same application into one tabbed window.

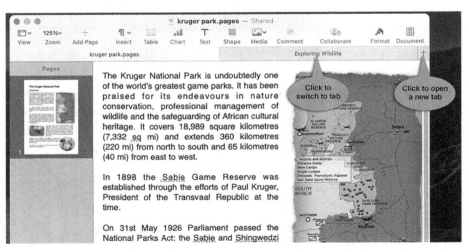

Click the tabs to switch between the tabbed windows, click the + sign on the right hand side to open a new tab.

Maps

Another great feature in MacOS Big Sur is the maps app. You'll find the maps app icon either on your dock or on launchpad.

With the Maps app, you can explore cities, places of interest, as well as finding directions to a particular destination.

Exploring Places

To find a place, click in the search field on the top left, then enter an address, name of a shop or location you're looking for.

You'll see a list of matching places appear down the left hand side. If your location is found on the map, you'll see an orange pin appear with the place name. Click a location's pin on the map for more info.

You can use the four icons at the top of the info sheet to place a call to the location's customer service line, open the location's website, create a guide, and share the location with someone or send it to your iPhone or iPad.

You can also plot a route from your current location. Click 'directions'.

185

Share a Location

To share a location with someone, click the location's pin on the map. Click the 'share' icon, go down to 'share', then select the app you want to use to share the location with. Eg you can send the location using mail, messages, airdrop, or you can add the location to your notes or reminders.

If you're sending the location using mail, messages or airdrop, select the person you want to send the location to.

Share a Map

To share a map, click the 'share' icon in the top-right corner of the info window.

From the drop down menu, select the app you want to share the map with. If you're sending the location using mail, messages or airdrop, select the person you want to send the location to.

Favourites

Click the location's pin, then click the three dots icon on the top right of the location's info card.

You'll see your favourite locations appear on the sidebar. Click a favourite on your sidebar to revisit.

Drop a Pin

Right click on the position on the map where you would like to drop a pin. Select 'drop pin'

Guides

The Guides feature is intended to provide expert recommendations for the best places to visit in a city, such as places to eat, shop, and places of interest to explore. Useful if you're visiting a city and want to find out where to eat, shop, or what to do. There are only a few cities such as Los Angeles, San Francisco, New York and Seattle that include this feature at the moment, but more will be added soon.

To view a guide on a city, type the city name into the search at the top left of the screen. Select the city name from the search results. If the city has guides you'll see them appear at the top of the info card for that city. Click 'see more' to view the whole list.

Click on any of the guides to view more information and see the location on the map

Select an attraction and you'll see the location appear on the map with an info card.

You can also create your own guides and share them with friends, family and colleagues.

To add a location to your own guide, click the three dots icon on the top right of the info card. Select the guide you want to add the location to. If you're creating a new guide, click 'new guide'.

Rename your guide. Right click the guide in the left hand pane, then select 'edit guide'. Type in a new name

Public Transport Routes

You can also check public transport in the local area. To do this click the maps icon on the top right, select 'public transport' from the menu.

You'll see bus and train routes appear on the map. Click on a bus or train station to see what services are running and when your next bus or train is due.

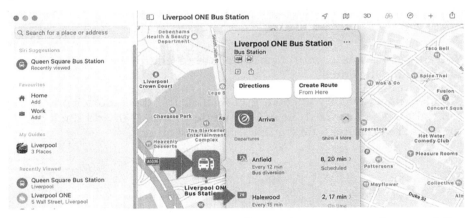

Find your service from the list. You'll see the route numbers and the times when they're due. Click on the route number to see the full route.

Here you'll see the full route of the service, indicated on the map in blue.

Driving Directions

You can type the name of the city or venue you are looking for in the search field at top centre of the screen. You can also enter postal/zip codes to find specific areas.

Click 'directions' icon on the top right of the screen.

Select the 'car' icon to plot driving directions. Type in your location and your destination in to the fields shown below.

Sometimes the maps app will come up with more than one route. These will be listed down the right hand side. Click on the route you want to take. Click the small right arrow to expand the route to show turn-by-turn directions.

You'll see the route shown in blue on the map.

To send the map to your iPhone or iPad, click the share icon on the top right, then from the drop down menu, select your device.

Walking Directions

Walking directions are useful if you're trying to find your way to a shop or location in a city.

Click 'directions' icon on the top right of the screen.

Select the 'person' icon to plot walking directions. Type in your location and your destination in to the fields shown below.

Click the small right arrow next to your route to show turn-by-turn directions.

Useful to transfer to your iPhone when walking around the location.

Look Around

To take a closer look at a place, click the binocular icon on the top right

Drag the map left and right or drag the image in the window to look around.

Explore in 3D

Using the satellite map, you can view cities in 3D. Type the name of the city into the search field on the top left of the screen.

Select the maps icon, then 'satellite' from the selections.

Click '3D' on the bottom right hand side. Use the '+' & '-' icons on the bottom right to zoom in and out of your map. Click and drag your mouse to move the map around the screen.

Look Inside

Apple have started adding indoor features to their maps app. This includes interior layouts and maps of airports, shopping malls and other venues. Just click 'look inside' link.

Not all locations have this feature yet.

Apple Books

Formerly known as iBooks, Apple Books allows you to download and read ebooks.

To open Apple Books open launchpad and select the Apple books icon.

Once Apple Books opens, you'll see the main screen. Let's take a look at the different sections. Along the top of your screen you'll see a toolbar, here you can select your library, bookstore, audio book store, and the search field.

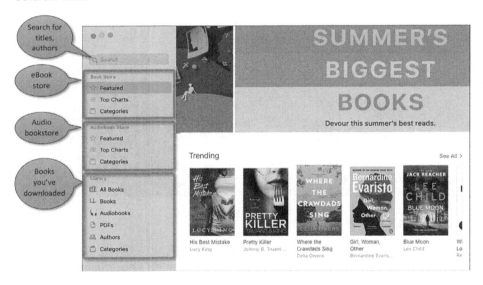

To search for more books, click the search field on the top left.

Once you have found a book you want, click on the book cover.

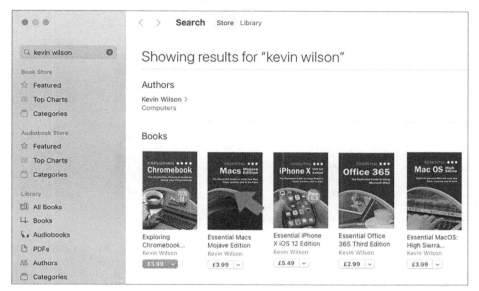

You'll see a description of what the book covers or is about, details about the book such as sample pages, technical stats, reviews and write ups.

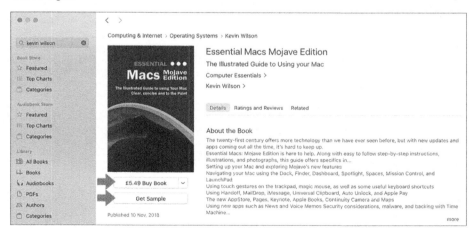

Click 'get sample' to see inside the book.

Click the price to buy the book, this will download it and add it to your library.

Enter your Apple ID email address and password if prompted. Click 'buy' on the confirmation dialog box.

You can find all your books that you have purchased, in your library section. Select 'all books' from the grey panel on the left hand side.

Double click on the book covers to open the books.

Once the books are open, you can 'turn the pages' by swiping two fingers left or right across the trackpad on your macbook. If you are using a mouse, click the left or right arrows on the edge of the screen to turn the page.

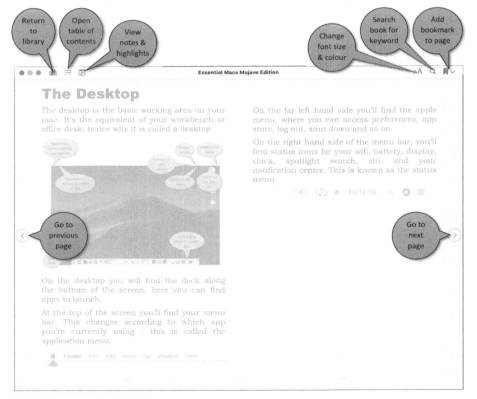

You can also add notes and highlight parts of the book. Click and drag your mouse across the text you want to highlight, then right click on the selection.

From the popup menu select a colour to highlight the text.

To add a note, click 'add note' then type your note into the post-it that appears. To see all your notes click 'view highlight or notes' icon on the tool bar at the top.

You can also add bookmarks. To do this, on the page you want to bookmark, click the bookmarks icon on the top right of the screen.

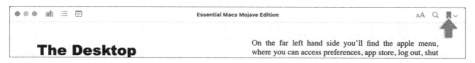

To return to a bookmark, click the small down arrow next to the bookmarks icon on the top left. Select your bookmark from the drop down list.

Notes

You can take notes using the notes app. To launch notes, open launchpad and select the notes icon.

When you open the notes app, you'll see the main screen. Here you can see your notes you have created either on your iPad/iPhone or on your Mac - these are listed in the centre pane.

On the right hand pane, you'll be able to edit a note you've selected in the centre pane.

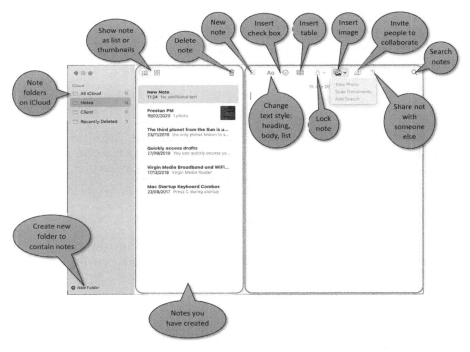

Click on a note in the list to view. Click the 'new note' icon to create a new note. There's an option to pin your most used notes to the top of the notes app for quick access to lists and other frequently used notes. To do this, right click on the note in the list and from the popup menu, click 'pin note'. This will make sure it stays at the top of the list. You can also insert an image - drag and drop from finder, or use your iPhone.

Tables can also be added to individual notes for better organization. Open an existing note or create a new one. Click on the 'insert table icon' on the toolbar.

You can also add check boxes to make 'to do' lists. To do this, open a new note or select one to edit. To add the check box, click the check box icon on the toolbar.

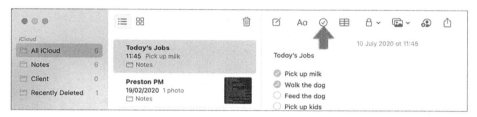

Once you have completed the task, click the circle next to it, to mark the task as complete.

You can also add photos. Select the photo icon from the toolbar. From the drop down menu select 'take photo' to take a photo with your iPhone or iPad, select 'scan documents' to scan a doc with your iPad, or 'add a sketch' to use your pencil on your iPad to create a sketch.

To invite people to collaborate on your note, click the invite icon.

Calendar

This utility is useful for storing all your friends email addresses, phone numbers, etc. These can be synced with your iPad or iPhone. To open calendar, select launchpad from the dock, then click the calendar icon.

I find it easiest to view the calendar in month view as shown below.

Adding an Event

The quickest way to add a new event is to click on the plus sign, then type in your event, date, time and location.

As you can see calendar has interpreted the event and added an entry into your calendar. Click on the suggestion show.

Your appointment will show up on your calendar. Select the calendar from the icon on the left. Eg this is a family event, so I'll add it to the family calendar. If it's a work appointment, select 'work'.

You can also add a location, click 'add location'. If you want to set a reminder, click 'add alert'. If this is a repeating event, click 'repeat', then select the frequency - daily, weekly, monthly etc.

Create a Calendar

You can create calendars to keep your appointments organised. All work appointments go in the 'work' calendar, personal appointments go in 'home, etc. You can also create other calendars. To do this, click the 'file' menu, then select 'new calendar'.

The new calendar will appear in the sidebar on the left, type in a meaningful name.

Export Calendar

Select the calendar you want to export from the side panel. Click the file menu, then select export, then click 'export' on the slideout. In the 'where' field, select the folder you want to save the calendar into.

Import Calendar

Click the file menu, then select 'import'. From the popup dialog box, select the calendar file you want to import. Click 'import'.

Add an Event from Email

Apple Mail scans your emails for possible events, meaning in some emails informing you of or inviting you to events, you'll see an option to add the event to your calendar. To add to your calendar, tap 'add' circled below/top-right.

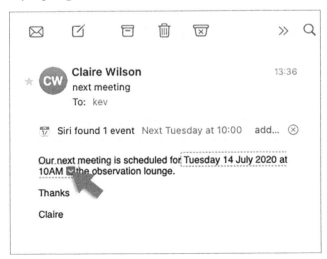

A window will appear detailing the event. Edit the title if necessary, select the calendar to add the event to eg 'work'.

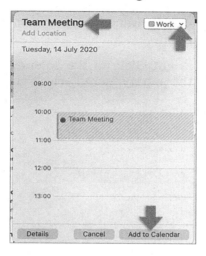

Click 'details' if you need to add reminders etc,. Click 'add to calendar' to add event.

Subscribing to Public Calendar

To add a public calendar go to the file menu and select 'new calendar subscription'.

Then give it an appropriate name and enter the address as shown above. Some sample addresses are below. These are public holidays. The first is public holidays in the UK, the second public holidays in the US.

```
webcal://ical.mac.com/ical/UK32Holidays.ics
```

```
webcal://ical.mac.com/ical/US32Holidays.ics
```

Sharing Calendars & Creating Public Calendars

You can share calendars with friends, family and colleagues. This is useful if you have events or appointments that people in a team or group need to know about.

To share a calendar, right click on the calendar in the sidebar you want to share. From the pop up menu, select 'share calendar'.

Select the people you want to share your calendar with. Start typing the person's name, then select the contact from the suggestions that appear. Do this with all the names you want to add.

If you want to make the calendar public, that is anyone with a link can view it, click the check box next to 'public calendar'. You'll see a URL appear. This is the link people will use to view the calendar. Click the icon next to the link to share it with people via email or social media.

Image Capture

Image capture is useful for importing images from scanners and some cameras. You can find the image capture app in finder/applications and on your launchpad.

Down the left hand side of the window you will see a list of your installed devices; cameras and scanners. Click on the device name to select it.

Along the bottom, select the directory you want to save the scanned image to, then select the scan size. To start the scan, click 'scan' on the right hand side.

If you need to change resolution, scan name or image format (png or jpg), select 'show details'.

Photobooth

This is probably the most entertaining app that comes pre-installed on a Mac. I had the kids entertained for hours. You can find photobooth on your launch pad.

Photobooth allows you to use your Mac's on-board camera to make face distorting images; pull a funny face or key out the background and find yourself underwater, on the moon, or a roller coaster.

Click the red camera icon in the middle of the tool bar along the bottom to take a picture.

You can also record video, if you select the video icon on the left hand side.

The fun part is when you get to the effects. Click 'effects' on the right hand side of the screen.

206

Have a look at the different effects below in the 9x9 grid. You can move around in the frame, or pull a funny face.

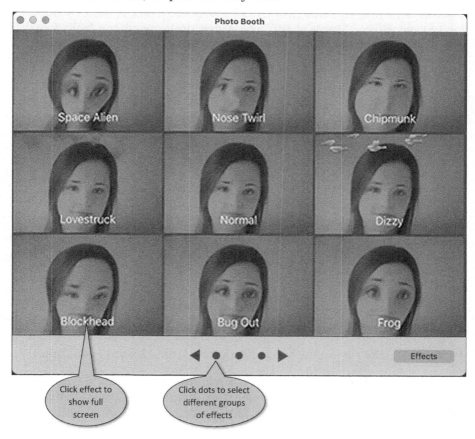

Click effect to show full screen

Click dots to select different groups of effects

You can select different types of effects, from the distorted mirrors, shown above, to highlight effects or keyed backgrounds.

To do this, click on the dots along the bottom of the window, highlighted above, to browse through the different effects.

Have fun.

DVDs & Blu-rays

MacOS still has the ability to play DVDs but has a lack of support for blu-ray discs. Many of the new Macs no longer have built in DVD drives so you'll need to buy an external USB DVD or Blu-ray drive.

To play a Blu-ray, you'll also need to buy a piece of software called *Aiseesoft - Blu-ray Player*. You'll be able to download it from this website:

www.aiseesoft.com/blu-ray-player

Plug the drive into a spare USB port and insert the disc.

To watch a Blu-ray, open Aiseesoft Blu-ray player from launchpad.

To watch a DVD open DVD player. If you're using Mojave, Catalina or Big Sur, DVD player no longer appears on launchpad or the applications folder. To open DVD player, if it doesn't open automatically, click spotlight search on the top right of the screen. Then type:

dvd player

From the spotlight search results 'top hits', click 'dvd player'.

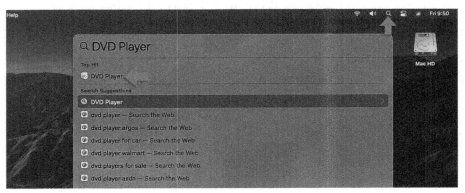

Once DVD player has started, your DVD will begin and will usually go to the DVD menu.

Lets take a look at the control panel at the bottom of the movie window.

Select the play movie option on your DVD menu to begin your movie.

Press **ctrl - cmd - F** on your keyboard to view in full screen mode. Press they key combo again to exit full screen mode.

To skip chapters in full screen mode, move your mouse pointer and you'll see a control bar appear on the bottom.

Here, you can also return to the menu, adjust volume, skip/play/ pause or stop movie.

Voice Memos

You can record audio using your Mac's built in mic or a bluetooth external mic. You can record voice memos, meetings, and lectures.

You'll find the voice memo app on your launch pad.

Lets take a look at the main screen. Here you can see your previous recordings listed down the left hand side. Any recording you select here will appear in the panel on the right hand side of the screen.

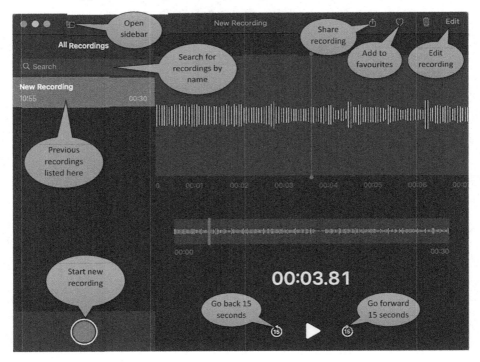

Click the play button in the panel on the right to playback the recording.

Recording Memos

To record a memo, simply click the red record button on the bottom left of the screen.

The memo app will start recording. You'll see a wave form appear in the middle of the screen to indicate the app is picking up audio.

To pause a recording temporarily, click the pause icon on the left. To stop the recording, click 'done'.

Your memo will appear in the list on the left hand side of the main screen.

Renaming Memos

The first thing you should do with a new voice memo recording is give it a meaningful name. The last thing you want is every memo called 'new recording.

To demonstrate this, we'll rename the voice memo we just recorded. Select the voice memo from the list on the left hand side.

Select the file menu on the to left. From the file menu, select 'rename'.

Delete the default text, then type in a meaningful name for the recording. Hit enter on the on screen keyboard to confirm the name.

Trim a Memo

You can trim the beginning and the ends of the memo voice recording. To do this, select the recording you want to trim from the list on the left hand side of the main screen. Then click edit on the top right of the grey panel on the right hand side.

Click the trim icon on the top right

Now to trim the beginning and ends of the clip, drag the yellow handles along the track until you get to the start and end points you want.

Click 'trim' when you're done.

News

The news app collects breaking stories from around the world and locally into one app, based on the topics you are interested in. You'll find the news app on your launch pad.

When you first start the app, you'll see a list of top stories, trending stories, and stories recommended for you. Scroll down the page, click on a story to read the details.

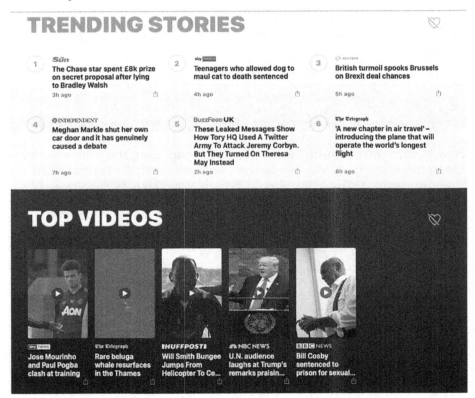

To open the side panel, tap the icon on the top left of the screen

From here you can select different news sources, magazines, newspapers and websites.

You can also search for specific channels. To do this, enter your search into the search field on the top left of the side panel.

Terminal

The terminal app provides text-based access to your Mac using a command-line interface allowing you to type in commands.

Opening Terminal

You'll find the terminal app in the 'utilities' folder in launchpad.

Click the terminal icon to start the app.

Here at the command prompt you type in commands...

All commands have three parts: the command name, flags, and arguments. The command name always comes first. The flags indicate a specific function of the command given, the arguments indicate the file, folder or process the command is working on.

```
command_name -flags [arguments]
```

Giving Commands

To give a command, type at the command prompt. For example to list the files in a directory. Type

```
ls -l
```

ls is the command, **-l** is a flag which returns a detailed list of the files.

Here are some common commands to try:

Command	Description
ls	List files and directories
ls -a	List all files and directories
ls -l	Detailed list of files and directories
mkdir <dir-name>	Create directory
cd <dir-name>	Change to directory
cd /	Change to root directory
cd ~	Change to home-directory
cd ..	Change to parent directory
find <name>	Find file <name> (use *)
pwd	Display the path of the current dir
cp <file> <destination>	Copy file to destination
mv <file> <destination>	Move file to destination
rm <file>	Delete file
rmdir <dir>	Delete directory
more <file>	Displays file a page at a time
head <file>	Displays first few lines of file
tail <file>	Displays last few lines of file
grep 'keyword' <file>	Search file for keyword
zip -r <archive> *	Zip files & folders in current directory
zip <archive-name> <files>	Compress files into zip archive
unzip <file-name>	Uncompress zipped file
nano <file-name>	Text editor
tree	Display directory tree

To create a folder use **mkdir**

```
mkdir documents
```

To copy a file use the **cp** command

```
cp earth.doc documents
```

This copies the file earth document to the documents folder.

217

Pages App

Pages is a desktop publishing and word-processing package that allows you to create all sorts of documents from letters to flyers

If you don't have these applications on your Mac, you can download them from the App Store.

Getting Started

To launch Pages, click the icon on your Launchpad.

Once Pages has opened, you can open a saved document, or click 'new document' to open a new one.

Double click on a template from the options, or select 'blank' to start from scratch.

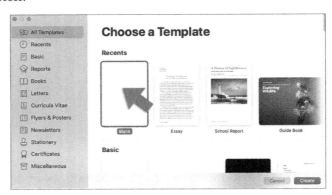

Once you have selected the template to use you will see the main work screen. Select the 'document' icon on the far right to edit document settings such as document margins, paper size, page orientation, sections - page numbering and bookmarks. Select 'format' to edit text styles, change font, text alignment etc.

Let's take a closer look at the main editing screen.

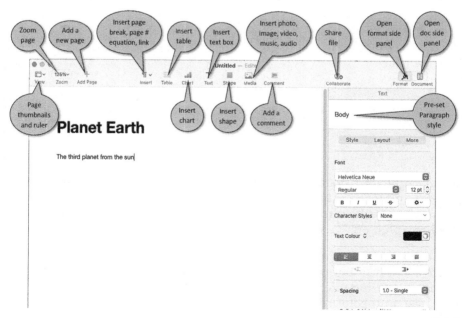

Formatting Text

To format text, select the text with your mouse. For example, I'm going to change the text 'planet earth' to a heading

Highlight your text with the mouse as shown above then click the 'format' icon on the top right. Select the small down arrow on the right hand side of the screen and click title from the menu that appears.

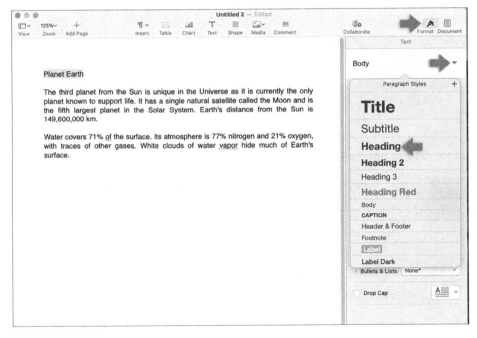

Formatting your document means laying it out in a style that is easy to read and looks attractive. This could involve changing fonts, making text bigger for headings, changing colour of text, adding graphics and photographs, etc.

For each document template you choose from the Template Chooser there are a number of pre-set paragraph styles. These are to help you format your document consistently, eg so all headings are the same font, size and colour.

Adding a Picture

The easiest way to add a picture is to find it in your finder window, then click and drag it into your document.

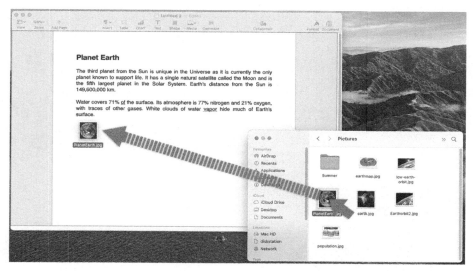

It might be helpful to position your finder window next to your document window as shown in the figure above.

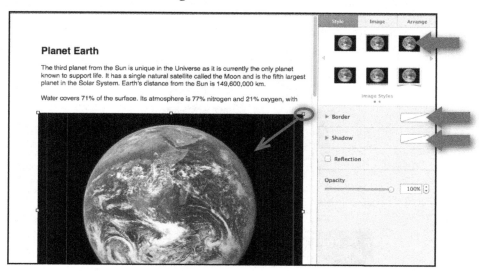

You can resize your image by clicking the resize handles, circled above, and dragging them. You can change the styles by adding borders and shadows by experimenting with the options in the style tab on the right hand side of the screen.

Chapter 4: Using Applications

Instant Alpha

If you look at the image we just added, you'll see it has a black background. To get rid of this you can use 'instant alpha'. First select your image.

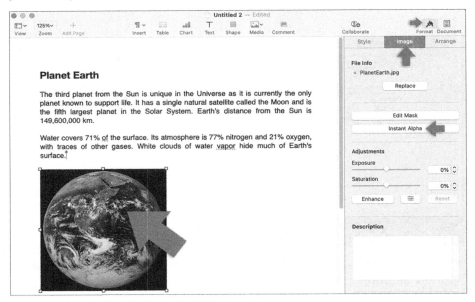

Click the 'format' icon on the top right then select the 'image' tab.

Click and drag your mouse in the black area around the image. This is the bit we want to get rid of. To remove any similar colours that are not initially deleted. On the image click your mouse on the area of the image and drag it slightly until it changes to grey. Click 'done'.

Saving

You can either save your work on your iCloud Drive or your local documents on your mac. Go to the file menu and select save...

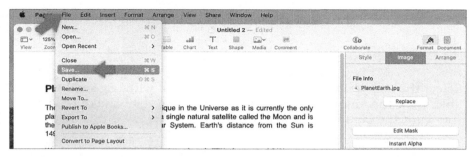

Give your document a name, then select the small down arrow to expand all the options.

Down the left hand side of the screen you will see some destinations where you can save your file. Select 'icloud drive', then select a folder on icloud drive, eg 'documents'.

The advantage of saving to your iCloud Drive is you can access and edit the documents you have just been working on, on your iPhone or iPad. Or even another mac.

Sharing and Collaboration

You can share your document with other people and invite friends and colleagues to collaborate and contribute to your document.

To do this, click the collaboration icon on the top right.

Select the app you want to share the document with. Eg send an email link, click the email icon. Set the permissions, use 'make changes' if you want the person to contribute.

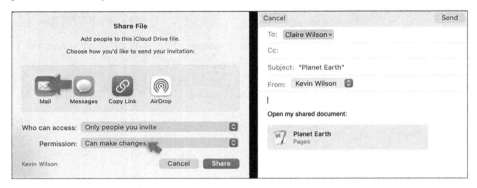

Enter the person's email address, click 'send'.

When the other person opens the document, you'll see their changes indicated with a marker.

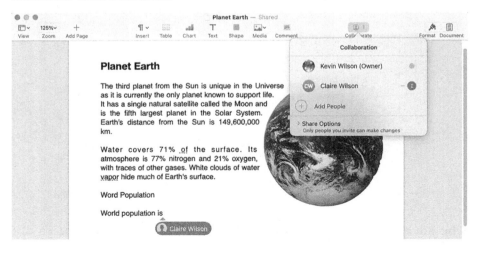

To change any settings, click the collaboration icon.

Keynote App

Keynote allows you to create multimedia presentations. If you don't have these applications on your Mac, you can download them from the App Store.

Getting Started

To launch Keynote, click the icon on your Launchpad.

Once keynote has loaded, you can select a saved file to open.

If you want to create a new presentation, click 'new document' on the bottom left hand side of the window. From here you can select from a variety of pre-designed templates with different themes, fonts and colours.

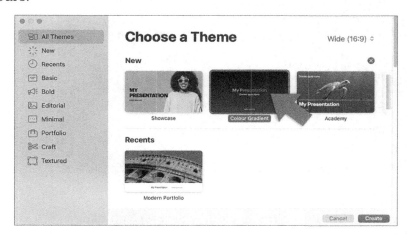

225

Chapter 4: Using Applications

Once you have selected a template you will see the main screen as shown below. This is where you can start building your presentation.

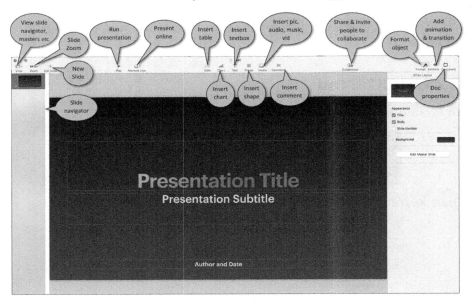

Editing a Slide

Double click in the heading field shown above and enter a heading eg 'Planet Earth'.

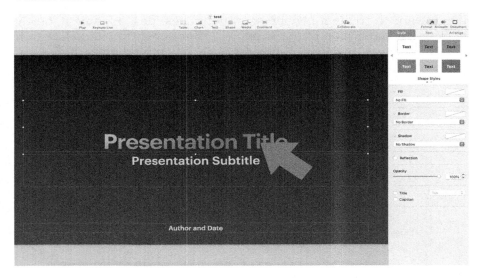

You can click and drag the heading wherever you like.

Adding a New Slide

Click the new slide button located on the bottom left of the screen.
Select a slide layout from the options that appear.

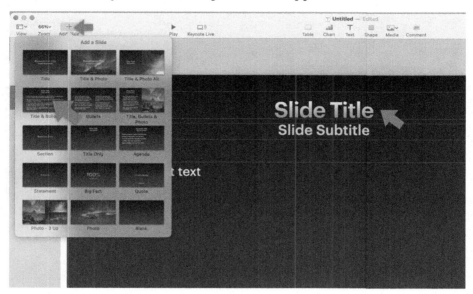

Add some text by double clicking on the text box that appears in the
slide.

Adding Media

The easiest way to add images and media to your slides is to find them
in your finder window then drag and drop them onto the slides where
the image is to appear.

Browse through, select the one you want, then drag and drop the image onto the slide. If you want photographs, you can drag and drop them from your photos app in the same manner as above.

It helps to drag your photos app window over to the right, as shown above so you can see your slide underneath.

You can insert videos and audio clips in the same way.

Animations

Animations allow you to make objects such as text or photographs appear in sequence or with an effect...

Select the object to animate. In this case, I want the bullet points to appear one by one.

Select the animate icon located on the top right corner of your screen

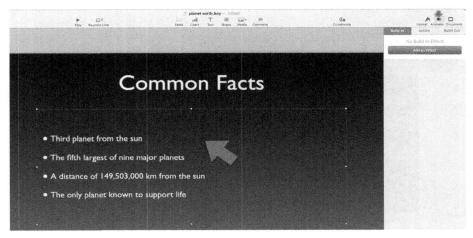

Select 'built in', then click 'add an effect'. Select an effect from the effects drop down menu, eg 'fly in'.

Then specify that you want the bullet points to appear one by one. Click the box under 'delivery' and select 'by bullet' from the drop down menu.

To see what the effect looks like, click 'preview'.

Slide Transitions

You can add transitions between slides. To do this, select the slide you want.

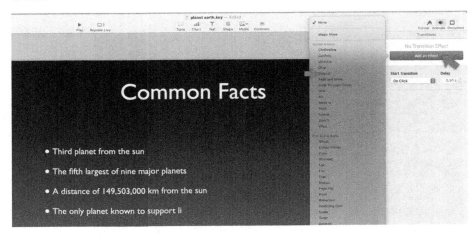

Select the 'animate' icon from the top right then click 'add effect'.

Formatting Text Boxes

Click text box to add shown below. Select the 'format' icon on the top right, then select the 'style' tab.

Now you can select a style, change the fill colour, border, opacity and reflection effects.

Enter some text into your textbox, and drag it into position on your slide.

You can format your text box by adding borders, changing fonts, changing the background colour, etc To format the border and fill click your text box and on the right hand side of the screen select style.

Formatting Text Inside Textboxes

To change the formatting of the text, for example to change the colour of the text or make it bold.

First select your text in the text box you want to change then click the text icon on the right hand side of your screen as shown below.

From here you can change the font, the font colour, size etc

Adding Styles to Textboxes

To change the background colour (also called fill colour) or add a nice border around the box click on your text box then select the format icon located on the top right of your screen

If you look down the right hand side you will see sections: 'Fill' allows you to change the background colour of the text box. 'Border' allows you to add fancy borders such as picture frames and coloured line borders. 'Shadow' allows you to add a drop shadow effect as if the text box is casting a shadow onto the slide.

To change the background colour of the textbox, click 'fill' and select a colour.

Also if you want to add a border, under the border section click where it says 'no border' as shown above and change it to 'picture frame'.

Click the 'choose frame style' button circled above and select a picture frame style from the menu that appears.

Change the size by moving the scale slider.

Saving

You can save your work onto your documents on your local mac or onto your iCloud Drive as with Pages. To do this, click the 'file' menu on the top left, then select 'save'.

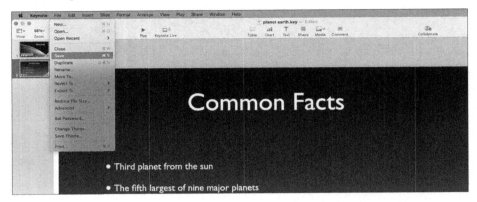

Give your document a name, then select the small down arrow to expand all the options.

Down the left hand side of the screen you will see some destinations where you can save your file. Select 'icloud drive', then select a folder on icloud drive, eg 'documents'.

Numbers App

The Numbers App allows you to create spreadsheets to present and analyse data. If you don't have these applications on your Mac, you can download them from the App Store.

Getting Started

To launch Numbers, click the icon on your Launchpad.

Once Numbers has loaded, you can select a saved file to open. Or to create a new spreadsheet, click 'new document' on the bottom left hand side of the window.

From here you can select from a variety of pre-designed templates with different themes, fonts and colours.

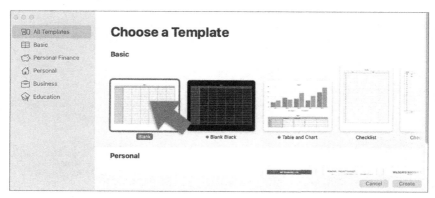

For this example use a blank sheet

Chapter 4: Using Applications

Once you have selected a template you will see the main screen as shown below.

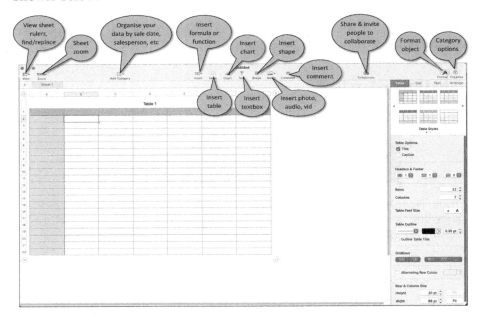

Along the top of the screen you'll see your toolbar. Here you can insert functions, images, tables and charts.

The 'format' icon on the right hand side opens up the sidebar and contains the tools needed to format text, rows, columns and the cells on your spreadsheet. The sidebar is split into tabs: table, cell, text, arrange, as shown below.

Building a Spreadsheet

To begin building your spreadsheet, enter the data into the cells. In this example we are going to build a basic invoice.

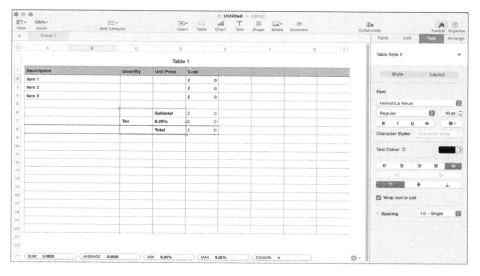

Entering Data

Enter the header cells into the grey row at the top of your spreadsheet. Then enter the rest of the data as shown below.

Change the total cells at the bottom to bold text. To do this, highlight them with your mouse, from the 'text' tab on the right hand side of your screen, click 'bold'.

Changing Data Types

Next highlight all the cells that will contain the prices for items, and make them a currency data type. Change it to Pound Sterling or US Dollar.

Do this by highlighting your cells as shown above, then from the cell tab on the right hand side, click in the dropdown box under 'data format' and select currency. Further down the tab you can change it to a specific currency depending on which country you are in.

Adding Formulas

Enter a formula to calculate the cost of each item. In the first cell under the heading 'cost' hit your equals sign to begin your formula. Click the cell under quantity, press the asterisk (*) then click the cell under unit price. This means you want to multiply the values in these two cells together.

Description	Quantity	Unit Price	Cost	
Item 1			= B2 ▾ × C2 ▾ ✗ ✓	
Item 2			£ 0	
Item 3			£ 0	
		Subtotal	£ 0	
	Tax	8.25%	£ 0	
		Total	£ 0	

Cost = Quantity * Unit Price.

238

Adding Functions

Now add a function to work out the total cost. For this one use the sum function to add all the values together.

Click in the cell next to subtotal and click the function icon on the tool bar at the top of the screen.

Select 'sum' from the drop down menu. The function will automatically highlight the values to add up.

If it doesn't click where it says D2:D5 this is the cells it will add up. Now select new the cells you want to add.

Saving

You can save your work onto your documents on your local mac or onto your iCloud Drive as with Pages.

Down the left hand side of the screen you will see some destinations where you can save your file. Take note of Documents under favourites - this is on your mac. Also take note of iCloud at the top, this saves onto your iCloud Drive.

The advantage of saving to your iCloud Drive is you can access and edit the documents you have just been working on, on your iPhone or iPad. Or even another mac.

Internet, Email & Communications

Your mac has a wealth of communication apps. MacOS has Safari for browsing the web, an email app to keep track of all your email correspondence. Plus an app for video chat called Facetime.

You can also use iMessage which is similar to the message app on your iPhone/iPad as well as AirDrop for sharing files and mac phone which syncs with your iPhone to allow you to answer calls right from your Mac.

There is also an address book called contacts that stores all your email addresses, phone numbers, Facetime IDs, mailing address and so on. This integrates nicely into your communication apps.

To help you better understand this section, take a look at the video resources. Open your web browser and navigate to the following site:

`videos.tips/sur-comms`

Lets take a look at the Safari web browser.

Using Safari to Browse the Web

Safari is the default web browser. Introduced in Big Sur is a new privacy report showing blocked trackers and privacy information on web pages. There is a new customisable start page allowing you to add favourite websites. You can also translate pages and grant access to web extensions for each website.

Launching Safari

You will find Safari's icon either on the dock at the bottom of the screen or on your launchpad

Click the icon to start the app. You'll land on Safari's customisable start page.

To customise, click the customise icon on the bottom right...

Customise your Homepage

Select your customisations from the popup menu. The list of sections on the popup list corresponds to the list of sections on the home page.

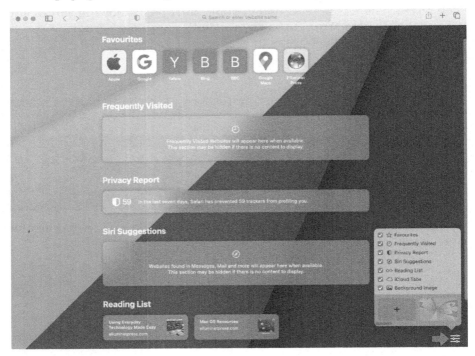

Select the check boxes to enable/disable the sections on the home page.

At the bottom of the popup click the + icon to choose a background image for your safari home page.

You can also scroll along the list to select a pre-installed background.

Using Safari

If for example, I wanted to find Elluminet Press's website, all you need to do is type it into the search bar. You can use a web address (URL) or type in keywords to do a Google search.

You can use this technique for anything you want to find. Just start typing it into the address bar.

Browsing Tabs

Tabbed browsing allows you to open multiple websites within a single window, using tabs as a navigational feature for switching between open websites.

To open a new browsing tab, click the + icon on the top right of the browser window.

To switch between the tabs, just click on the tab you want to switch to.

To close a tab, just click the small x that appears on the left of the tab.

To open a link in a new tab, hold down the command key while you click the link

Show all Browsing Tabs

To show all open tabs at once, click the 'show tab overview' icon on the top right.

Bookmarking Pages

Bookmarking pages allows you to save websites you visit frequently so you don't have to search for them or remember the web address. You can just click the site in the bookmarks side bar to revisit the page.

To bookmark the page you're currently on, click the share button on the top right.

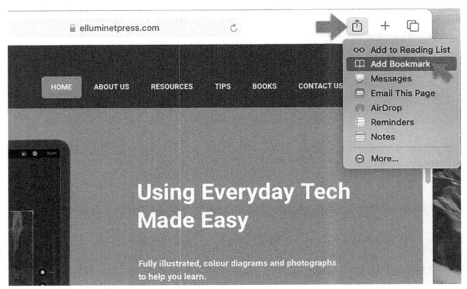

From the menu, select 'add bookmark'.

Now, under 'add this page to', select where you want to save the site to. Select either 'favourites' or 'bookmarks'.

Select 'favourites' to add the site to the favourites section of the 'start page'. Select 'bookmarks' to save the website to the bookmarks side panel, as shown below.

At the bottom of the dialog box, type in a name and description if necessary, then click 'add'.

Revisiting Bookmarked & Favourite Sites

If you saved the site to 'favourites', then you'll see the site in the 'favourites' section of the start page.

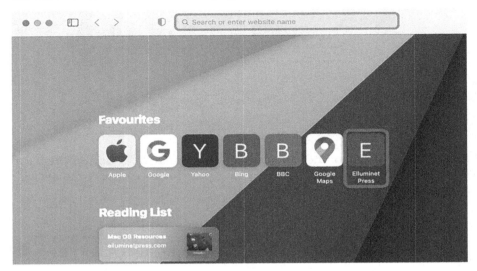

To return to a bookmarked site, click the 'sidebar' icon on the top left of the toolbar to open the panel. From the sidebar, click on the bookmarks tab on the top left.

Here you'll see a list of all the sites you have bookmarked. Click the site link to revisit the site.

You might need to expand the folders, do this by clicking the small triangle to the left of each folder, indicated with the small red arrow in the above screen.

Organising Bookmarks

You can also organise your bookmarks into folders. So for example, all my publishing websites I could put into a publishing folder. First, open the sidebar and select the bookmarks icon.

To create folders right click on the bookmark sidebar and select 'new folder'.

Give the folder a name. In this case I am naming it 'Publishing'.

Drag and drop your bookmarks into the folders, as illustrated below.

This helps to keep all your bookmarks organised and easy to find. You could have a folder for your work, interests, hobbies or sites you use to book your holidays/vacations.

Reading List

The reading list is where you can queue up a load of websites for reading later, useful when you are not connected to the internet all the time.

To add a site to your reading list, click the share button on the top right. From the drop down menu select 'add to reading list'.

To view the sites you've added to your reading list, click the 'sidebar' icon on the top left of your screen. Select the 'reading list' icon from the sidebar.

Downloads

Click the downloads icon on the top right of the screen. This icon only appears after you've downloaded something. Click the document to open, click the small magnifying glass icon next to the download to open it in finder.

You'll also find your downloads in the document stack on the bottom right of your dock.

Extensions

Safari extensions customise the way your browser works. You can add extensions to block adverts, and add extra functionality.

To install the extensions, open safari, click the 'safari' menu on the top left, then select 'Safari Extensions. The app store will open up with a list of extensions that are available.

To install any extension click 'get', then click 'install' to add the extension.

Now, you'll need to enable the extension. To do this, click the 'safari' menu, then select 'preferences'.

Click the 'extensions' tab.

On the left hand side, click the tick box next to the extension to enable it. Remove the tick to disable it.

To remove the extension select it from the panel on the left, then click 'uninstall'.

Privacy Reports

Safari uses its Intelligent Tracking Prevention to identify and block trackers advertisers use to track your web activity. On the toolbar you'll see a new icon you can click to see which trackers have been blocked on the current website.

You can also get a privacy tracking report. In safari, click the 'safari' menu, then select 'privacy report'.

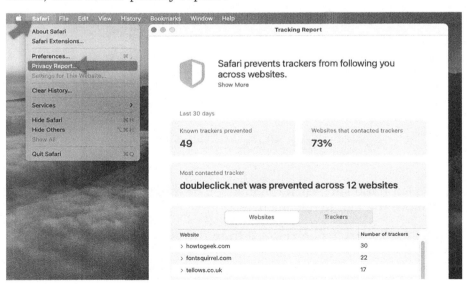

You'll see some stats. Click the 'websites' tab to see all the websites where trackers have been blocked. Select the 'trackers' tab to see a list of all the trackers that have been blocked and who they belong to.

Passwords

When you sign into a website or for the first time, you will receive a prompt asking you whether you want to save your login details.

Sign in, in the normal way - enter your username and password. Once you sign in successfully, Safari will prompt you to save the password.

Click 'save password'. This will save your password so you don't have to type it in each time.

To sign in the next time, just click in the username or password field.

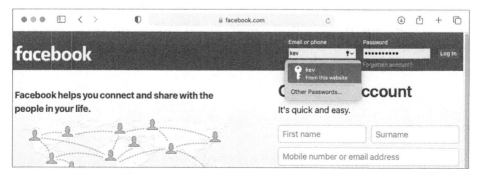

Select the username from the drop down list, click 'log in' or 'sign in'.

Managing Passwords

You can save passwords to your password list from various different websites so you don't have to remember them all. Top open password manager, click the 'safari' menu, then select 'preferences'. Select the 'passwords' tab and enter your Mac password.

Scroll down the list, select the site to view username and password saved for that site.

Click 'remove' to delete the saved password for selected site. To manually add a site, click add then enter the website address, username and password.

You can change the details for each saved password. Select the site, then click 'details'.

Website:	www.facebook.com
Username:	kev
Password:	sdf98743r*%$p00978

Edit the fields. Click the share icon to share username & password for selected site via airdrop.

Generate Automatic Strong Passwords

Strong passwords are a must these days. To help you generate good passwords, Safari can automatically generate them for you when you use it to sign up or open an account on any website - whether it's facebook, google, microsoft, yahoo and so on.

To start, go to the website where you want to sign up for an account. In this example I'm going to sign up to GMail.

Fill in the 'create account' form with your details. Click in the password field.

Click 'Use Strong Password'. Safari will automatically generate a strong password for you and save it into your passwords list.

The next time you need to sign into the site, just click in the password field and select the username for that site.

Autofill Forms

You can get safari to automatically fill in a form for you using your contact information. To set it up, open the 'safari' menu, and select 'preferences'. From the preferences window, select the 'autofill' tab.

Next to 'using information from my contacts' click 'edit'. Enter all your contact details.

This will enable you to select them when filling in a from on a website. On the form, click in one of the fields. You'll see a small contacts icon appear on the right hand side of the form.

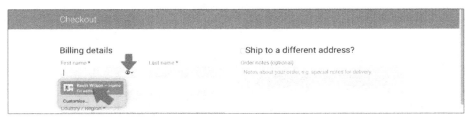

Click the icon, then select your contact from the list.

Billing details		Ship to a different address?
First name *	Last name *	Order notes (optional)
Kevin	Wilson	
Company name (optional)		
Country / Region *		
United Kingdom (UK)		
Street address *		
31 Main Street		

Apple Mail

Apple Mail, also known as the Mail App, is an email program included with Mac OS.

With Apple Mail, you can include all your email accounts in one app. These are listed in the sidebar down the left hand side of the screen. On the sidebar, you'll also see your mail boxes: inbox, sent, junk and so on for all the email accounts you've added.

In the middle pane, you'll see a list of email messages in the mail box you've selected from the sidebar. In the example below, 'inbox' is selected from the sidebar and the email messages are listed in the middle pane.

In the far right pane, you'll see a preview of the message you have selected from the middle pane.

To read the message in full, double click the message listed in the middle pane.

Email Threads

An email conversation that spreads across dozens of messages in your inbox is called a thread. Apple Mail organises your email messages by thread. Here in the demo below is an email conversation between Claire and me.

You can see in Claire's inbox below, her email conversation with me. In the reading pane you'll see the email conversation (or thread). To make things easier to explain, I've marked messages Claire has sent in green, and messages I've sent in blue. Notice the latest email is at the bottom of the thread.

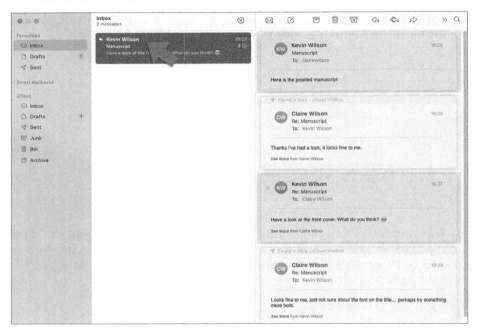

When you select the email conversation in the inbox (indicated above with red arrow) and click 'reply', you'll automatically reply to the latest message in the thread. To reply to a particular message in the thread, hover your mouse over the message, you'll see a small toolbar appear.

Click the 'reply' icon. Or if you want to delete it, click the bin icon.

You can turn this feature off, if you'd rather list all your emails in your inbox as they arrive. To do this, click the 'view' menu on the top left.

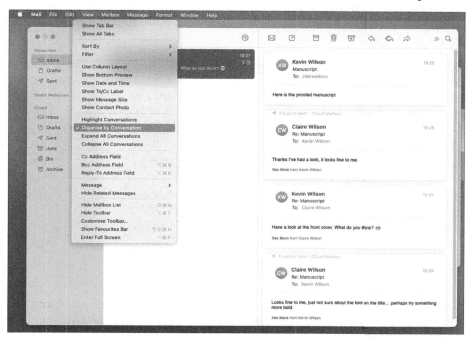

Select 'organise by conversation' to remove the tick.

Show BCC Field

If you want to send messages to multiple recipients, but you don't want everyone to see everyone else's email addresses, you can add the addresses to the BCC field. BCC stands for blind carbon copy and isn't enabled by default. To reveal the field, click the view menu then select 'bcc address field'.

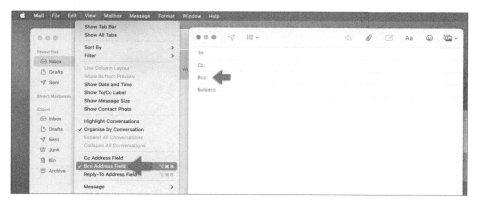

Replying to a Message

To reply to an email, select the email you want from your inbox, then click the 'reply to sender' icon on the top right. If you don't see the icons click the '>>' icon on the right.

Note there are two reply icons. The first icon allows you to only reply to the sender (in the to: field). The second icon allows you to reply to the sender and everyone else the message was sent to - so if the message was sent to multiple recipients in the to:, cc: or bcc: fields.

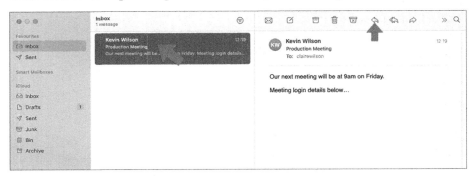

Type in your message at the top of the window that appears. Here you can craft your reply as you would a new email. See "Writing a New Email" on page 260.

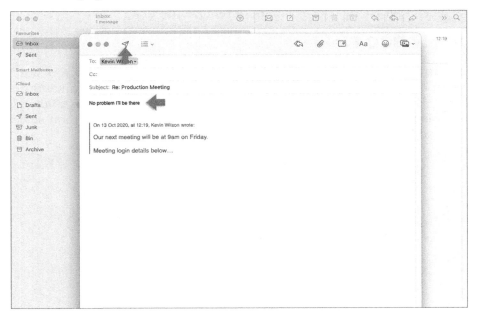

Click the send icon on the top left of the window.

Forward a Message

You can forward a message to another person. To do this, select the email you want to send to someone else, then click the 'forward' icon on the top right. If you don't see the icons click the '>>' icon on the right.

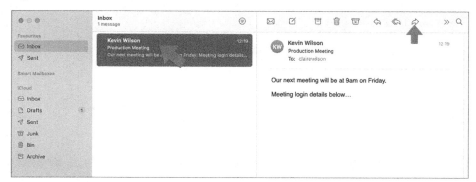

Enter the person's email address in the 'to:' field.

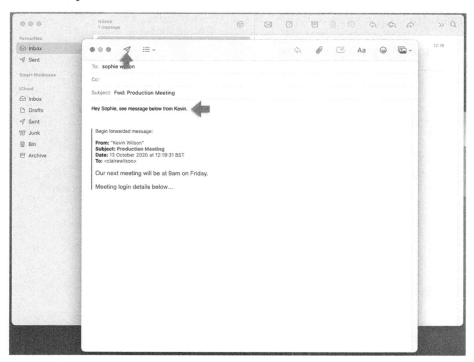

Add a message at the top of the email if you want to.

Click the send icon on the top left of the window to send your message.

Chapter 5: Internet, Email & Communications

Writing a New Email

To send a new email, click the 'compose new email' icon on the top left of your screen. A new blank email window will pop up.

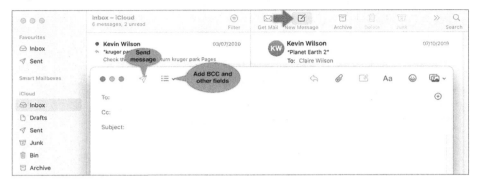

Enter an email address in the 'to' field. If you need to send the message to more than one person, add their email addresses to the CC field. If you don't want everyone else's email address to show up in everyone's copy of the email, enable the BCC field. Type a subject in to the 'subject' field, then type your message in the space underneath.

Formatting your Message

Click the font icon that looks like 'Aa', to reveal the formatting bar.

Select the tools from the formatting bar to format your text, change colour, size, alignment, and font. Remember to highlight the text you want to format first, if you've already typed it in. To add numbered lists or bullet points, click the 'bullet list & numbering' icon.

Add an Emoji

You can add emojis like the ones you see on iMessage, into your email messages. To do this, click the emoji icon on the toolbar.

From the drop down, select from the categories of emoticons along the bottom, you can choose smilies, animals, fruit, etc. Click the emoji you want to add

Add Attachment

Click the paper clip icon to add an attachment such as a PDF or word document, or a photo you downloaded. Select the file from the dialog box then click 'choose file'.

Add Photo from Photos App

If you want to add a photo from your photos app, click the photo icon to pull up your photo albums, as shown above. You can drag and drop any photo into your email to send along.

When you're ready to send your message, tap the send icon on the top left.

Mail Drop

MailDrop allows you to send large files by automatically uploading them to your iCloud drive, and then sending a link to the recipient so they can access the file without clogging up the mail server with large files. MailDrop uses your iCloud to store your files, and because iCloud is built into Mail, this means that anyone running Mail on their own Mac will have the file downloaded automatically, just as though it were an ordinary email.

Mail Drop will automatically upload large attachments to iCloud instead of your email provider ie Gmail, Yahoo, or Exchange etc.

If your recipient also uses Mail on a Mac, they'll be able to download the attachment normally, and if not, they'll get a download link that's accessible for 30 days. These attachments don't count towards your iCloud storage limits, which is great. Smaller attachments are sent as normal.

You can open and compose a new email as normal and attach a file. In this example the file is 161MB which is pretty large for an email attachment.

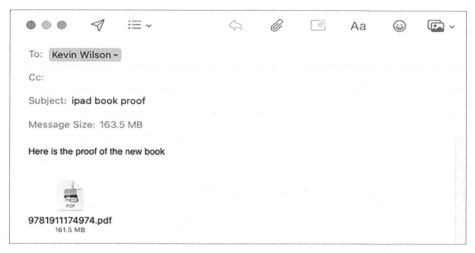

When your recipient receives the email, there will be a link that will allow them to download the attachment. If your recipient using a Mac, then they need to right click on the link then select 'save to downloads folder'. Go to the downloads folder in finder, then double click the file.

If your recipient is using a Windows PC, then they need to click on the attachment link in the email as shown below.

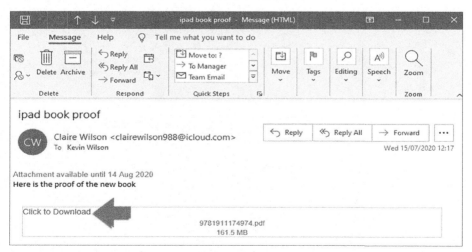

From the 'save as' dialog box select a folder to download the attachment to (eg downloads). This will download the attachment into the downloads folder. From here they can open and read the attachment.

Mail Markup

Markup provides a simple way of adding comments and annotations to file attachments in Mail and mostly works with photos or pdf documents.

If you send someone a photo for example, in an email you can activate markup mode, by clicking on a small pull-down menu that appears in the top-right corner of the image.

You can then annotate your image, type text, draw lines, circles and hand written notes on the image.

Below is an explanation of what all the different icons do.

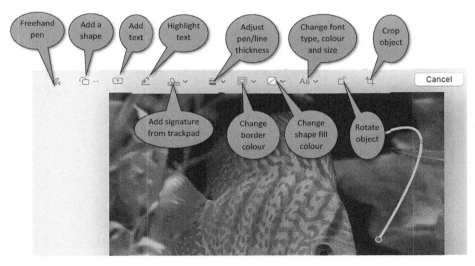

Click the 'freehand pen' icon.

Now you can draw or write on your photograph.

Try some of the other tools such as a shape, add some text. Once you have finished annotating your image click 'done'.

If you don't see the markup pop-up menu, you may need to enable it. To do this, click the apple menu on the top left of the screen, then select 'system preferences'. Double click 'extensions'.

Click actions, then select the markup checkbox.

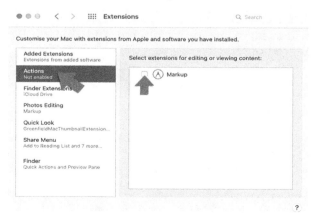

Dealing with Spam & Junk Mail

We all get junk mail - those annoying messages trying to sell you things and just clutter up your inbox with rubbish. Apple Mail has a spam filter where you can filter out these messages.

To enable junk mail filtering, open Apple Mail and go to the 'mail' menu. Select 'preferences'.

Select the 'junk mail' tab. Click the tick box next to 'enable junk mail filtering'.

Now occasionally, the junk mail filter will catch legitimate emails, so it's best to move them to the junk mail folder.

To do this, select 'move it to the junk mailbox'. This will keep your inbox clean and move junk to the junk mailbox.

This means that you can check the junk mail box from time to time to check which messages are being filtered and that no important ones have been filtered out.

Contacts

This is your address book and stores all your email, phone numbers, and addresses that you can access from the contacts app itself or through your email, FaceTime, or iMessage.

You'll find the contacts app on your dock, or launchpad. Click the icon to open the app.

You can create contacts, add email addresses and phone numbers. These contacts are synced with all your Apple devices; iPhone, iPad etc.

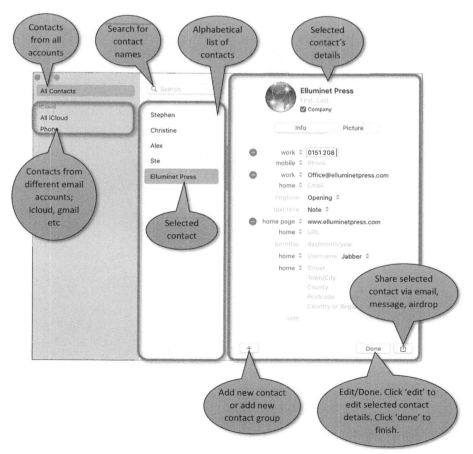

Add a Contact from Scratch

To add a new contact, click the plus sign on the bottom of the contacts window. Select 'new contact' from the drop down menu.

Enter the contact's details - first, last name, phone, email, address and any other information you have in the fields that appear.

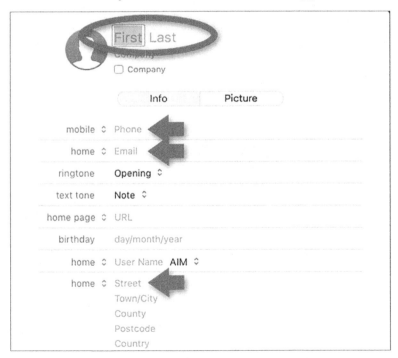

Click 'done' on the bottom right when you're finished.

Creating Groups

Groups make it easier to send an email to several different people. This group can be a team. In this example, I'm going to create a group called 'production team' and will contain a list of email address in my team. To create a group, click the plus sign at the bottom, and from the drop down select 'new group'. An untitled group will appear on the left hand side - type in a name.

Now you can drag and drop your contacts into the group.

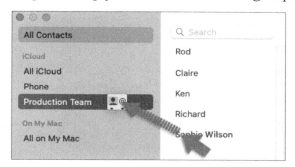

Now when you start a new email, you'll be able to type the group name into the 'to' field, rather than having to add all the email addresses manually.

Add Email Contact from Apple Mail

The easiest way to add someone's email address from an email message is to click on the small down-arrow next to the person's name in the email header, as shown below.

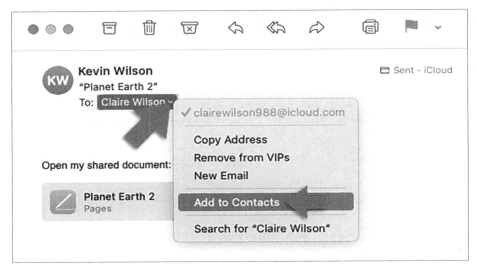

From the popup menu select 'add to contacts'.

This will automatically create an entry in your contacts list with the sender's name and email address from the email you have open.

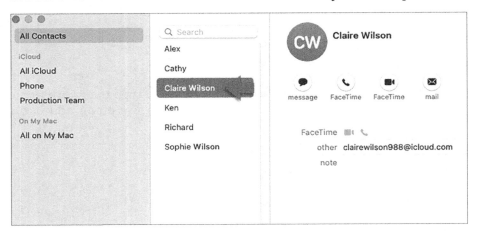

Take a look at the video demos. Open your web browser and navigate to the following website

videos.tips/sur-comms

Facetime

When you open Facetime, you will be prompted to sign in if you haven't already done so.

Placing Video Calls

Once Facetime has opened, you'll see in the main window a preview of your camera. On the left hand side you'll see a darkened panel where you'll find a list of contacts you've called or received calls from.

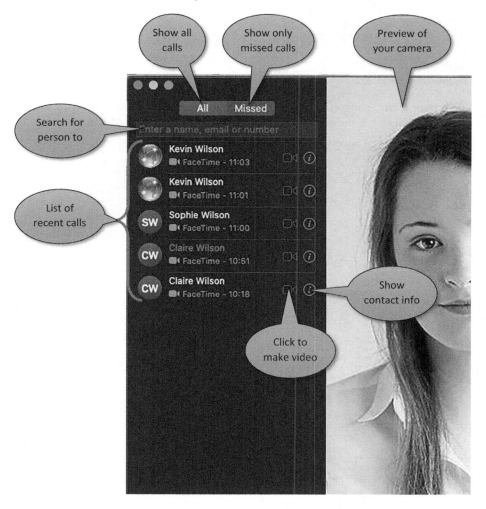

To make another call to the contact, click the camera icon next to their name in the list. Wait for them to answer.

Calling Someone New

To call someone new, start typing the contact's name you want to Facetime into the search field on the top left of the screen. If the name is in your contacts, then it will appear underneath. Click on their name in the list that appears.

Two green buttons will appear on the bottom left of your screen. Select 'video' to make a video call, select 'audio' to make a voice call.

Wait for the other person to answer...

Answering Calls

When a call comes in on your mac, you'll see a notification on the top right with a preview of your camera. *Note, no one will be able to see your camera until you accept the call.*

You'll see the name of the person calling on the left hand side of the notification window. Click 'accept' to receive the call, or 'decline' if you're busy or don't want to talk .

Now in the centre of the screen you'll see an image of the person you're calling. On the bottom right of the screen you'll see a preview of your own camera.

Press *CMD CTRL F* for full screen mode on your Mac.

Group FaceTime

To call a group, type the names of the contacts you want to add to your group into the search field on the top left of the screen. Select the names from the drop down menu as they appear.

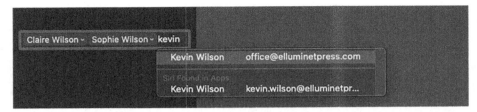

At the bottom you'll see two green buttons. Click 'video' to start a video chat. Click 'audio' to start a voice call.

Now, wait for everyone to answer.

You'll see your camera on the bottom right. Everyone else in the chat will appear in their own window. When a person starts talking their window will enlarge.

Message App

iMessage allows you to send media rich text messages to other iPhones, Macs and some other smart phones. You can find iMessage on your Dock at the bottom of the screen

You can send a new message by clicking on the new message icon, then in the new message window click the + sign to add your recipients.

From the drop down, select the contact from the list.

Sending New Messages

The message window will open up. Type your message in field at the bottom of the screen. You'll see a message transcript in the main window.

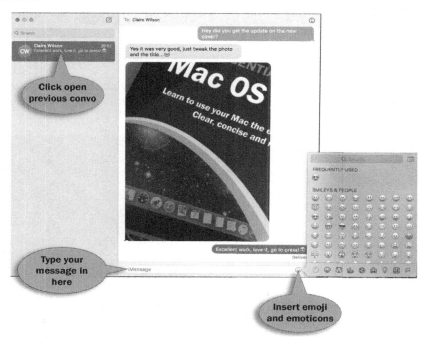

Click on the smiley face on the right hand side of the message field to add your emojis.

In the demo below, you can see the user on the left, is using iMessage on an iPhone, and is in conversation with the user on the Mac.

Sending Files

You can send files in your messages. To do this, click and drag a file, photo, or video from the desktop or finder directly into the message window.

Hit return to send your file.

Memojis

Memoji have made their way over to the mac, however at the moment they are a bit limited compared to the iPhone 10/11 and iPad Pro. You can still create and edit a Memoji and express yourself with Memoji stickers.

To get started click on the icon to the left of the text field. Select 'Memoji Stickers'.

To send, select any of the Memojis. Press enter to confirm.

To create a Memoji, click the three dots icon on the top left then select 'new Memoji'.

Run through the features listed down the left hand side of the window to create your Memoji. Click 'done'.

Message Effects

You add various effects to your messages such as fireworks, balloons, confetti, and lasers.

To send a message with an effect, type in your message, then click the icon on the left of the message box. Select 'message effects' from the drop down menu.

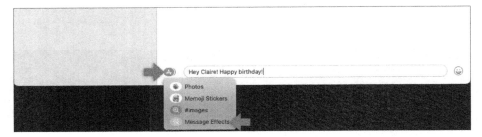

Select an effect from the options along the bottom of the window.

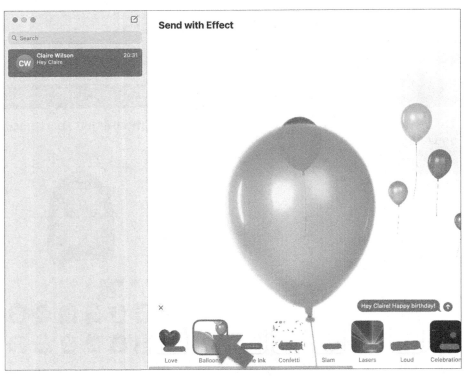

Press enter to send the message.

Try some of the other effects.

Air Drop

AirDrop is a service that enables users to transfer files to another supported devices ie Mac computer and iPad or iPhone without using email or a USB stick or external hard drive.

From Finder

You can airdrop a file from finder to any nearby device. To do this, open finder and navigate to the file you want to share.

Right click on the file, go down to 'share' then select 'airdrop' from the slide out menu.

Your Mac will detect nearby devices with airdrop enabled. Click the one you want to send the file to.

On the device, you'll see the file pop up.

In Safari

To airdrop a webpage from safari, navigate to the page you want to share, then click the 'share' icon on the top right. Select 'airdrop' from the slideout menu.

Select the device you want to share the page with.

If you have trouble sending/receiving, make sure the person you're sharing with is in your contacts, or set airdrop sharing to receive from anyone. You'll find the airdrop settings on control center.

Select 'everyone'.

Mac Phone

You can answer calls on your Mac if you have an iPhone. For this feature to work, you'll need to be connected to the same WiFi network, and signed in with the same iCloud account on both your Mac and iPhone. Then you'll need to enable the feature. On your iPhone, open the settings app and select 'phone'.

Turn on 'Calls on Other Devices'. You'll see the other Apple devices you'll receive your iPhone calls on.

Now, on your Mac, open the FaceTime app. Go to the preferences menu on the top left. Make sure 'Calls from iPhone' is selected.

Whenever you are on your Mac and your iPhone rings, you can pick up the call. You'll see a notification appear on the top right of the screen.

Click 'accept' to answer the call.

Using Multimedia

Photos has more features that are similar to the Photos app on the iPad and iPhone borrowing some of the same style of operation.

You can import photos from your iPhone and sync them with your Photos library as well as import them from a digital camera.

You can create some very nice looking photo books, greetings cards and slide shows all with your own photographs.

Photos also has features such as intelligent scene detection, face, place and object recognition and will automatically categorise your photos allowing you to search using people's names, place names, and objects.

There is also a 'memories' feature, that will automatically group your photos into slideshows for you to enjoy and share with your friends.

To help you better understand this section, take a look at the video resources. Open your web browser and navigate to the following site:

videos.tips/sur-mm

Photos App

The Photo App is a great way to store, view and manipulate your photographs. You can create albums and slide shows, you can email a photo to a friend, post them onto Facebook, you can even put together your own album send it to apple and they will print you out a copy and post it to you, these are great for family albums or wedding albums and other special occasions.

To open the Photos App, click the icon on the dock.

Once the app opens, you'll see all the photos that are on your Mac. Along the top of the window you'll see a toolbar.

Down the left hand side you'll see the sidebar. Under the library section, you'll be able to select 'photos' to view all the photos on your mac.

Select 'people' to view photos featuring people. The Photos App scans your photos for faces and creates a 'people album' for each person it finds.

Select 'places' to view a map showing the different places your photos were taken.

You'll also be able to see photos you've most recently added ('recents'), and photos you've imported from a digital camera ('imports').

Further down the sidebar you'll also see any albums you've created.

283

Importing your Photos

Most digital cameras connect to your computer using a USB cable, as shown below.

Open photos from launch pad and connect your camera. Photos will detect the camera connected and open up the import screen.

I found it best to delete them off the camera once imported into the Photo library. This means I have a clean camera for the next time I want to take photographs.

To do this, click the tick box next to 'delete items after import'. This helps eliminate duplicate photographs in the library.

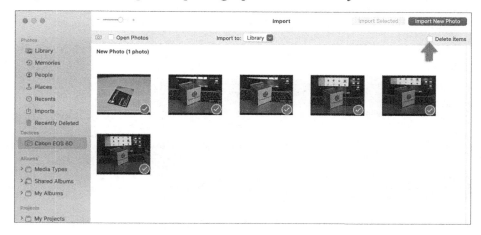

Now select 'imports' from the 'photos' section of the sidebar on the left hand side of the screen.

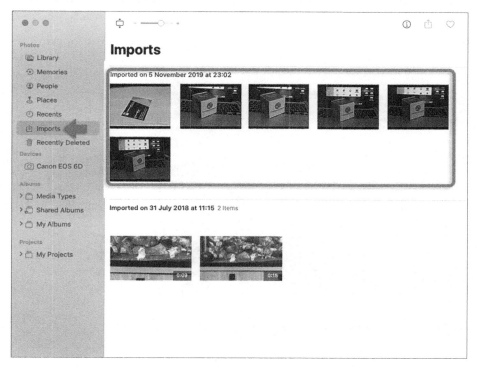

Scroll down, you should now be able to see all the photos you have just imported.

Manipulating & Adjusting Photos

A common problem I have come across, when taking photographs with a pocket digital camera, is sometimes photos can come out a bit dark.

To edit the photo, double click on it. Click 'edit' on the top right of the screen.

Select 'adjust' from the three options at the top of the screen.

Down the right hand side of the screen, you'll see a list of operations you can perform on your photograph.

For example, to change the brightness of the image, select 'adjust' from three options on the top, centre of the screen.

Under the adjustments on the right hand side, you'll see one called 'light'. Underneath you'll see a gradient going from a dark image to a light image and a slider somewhere in the middle. Click and drag this slider toward the light, to lighten the image.

Under the 'light' adjustment, select 'options'. Here, you can adjust the exposure - how bright the image is, you can adjust highlights - the bright areas, shadows - the dark areas, and contrast. To adjust drag the blue sliders left and right.

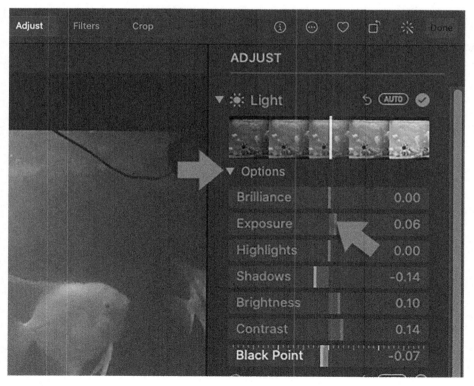

You can do the same for the 'color'; saturate and desaturate the colours. You can also click 'auto' on these adjustments and photos app will make a guess.

If you scroll further down the adjustment controls, you'll see some more advanced features.

You can change the white balance, this is good for adjusting photos that have a distinctive orange or blue tone to them.

Neutral gray is usually one to use, however if you are adjusting a portrait of someone, click this box and change it to 'skin tone'.

If you scroll further down the adjustment options, you'll see some more advanced features.

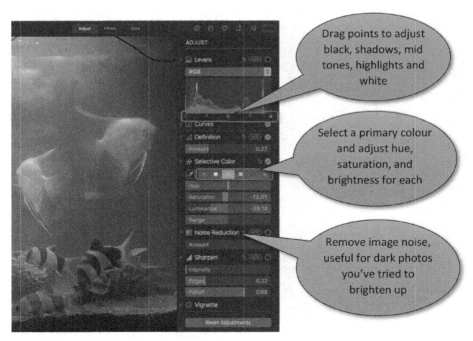

Drag points to adjust black, shadows, mid tones, highlights and white

Select a primary colour and adjust hue, saturation, and brightness for each

Remove image noise, useful for dark photos you've tried to brighten up

Click and drag the sliders underneath the names of the effects to adjust the photograph.

Adding Filters

Filters give your photograph a predefined look, such as changing your photo to a sepia or black and white look; make the colours more vivid, warm or dramatic.

Double click on your image and select 'edit' from the top right.

Select 'filters' from the options on the top centre of the screen.

Down the right hand side you'll see some filters. Click on the icons to apply the filter.

Click 'done' to save.

Creating Folders and Albums

The photos app allows you to organize your photos into albums (shown in green). You can in turn organise all your albums into folders (shown in blue).

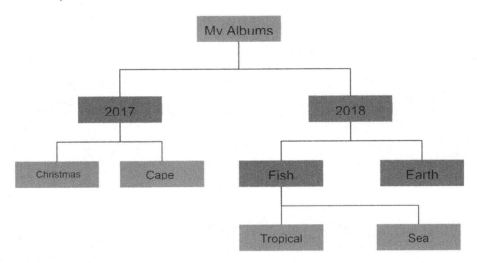

To create a blank folder or album, hover your mouse pointer over 'my albums'. Click the '+' sign that appears. From the popup menu select 'folder' to create a new folder.

I'm going to create a folder called '2017' to store my albums from that year. So type in '2017'.

Now, you can't create albums within albums, but you can organize your albums into folders.

Inside the '2017' folder, I'm going to create an album called 'cape'. Hover your mouse over the '2017' folder, click the '+' icon that appears. Select 'album' from the popup menu.

Type in the album name. Eg 'Cape'.

Follow the same procedure to create other albums and folders as needed.

Adding Photos to Albums

To add photos to your albums. Select 'library' from the 'photos' section of the side panel on the left hand side. Then select 'all photos' from the toolbar on the top of the window.

Select the photos you want to add - hold down the cmd key on your keyboard to select multiple photos. Click and drag the photos into the albums on the left hand panel under the 'albums' section of the side panel.

Places

Photos App will tag your photos and record where your photo was taken, this is called geo tagging. If you have GPS and location services set on your iPhone, the photos app will tag the photographs with the location.

Select 'places' from the sidebar on the left hand side of your screen.

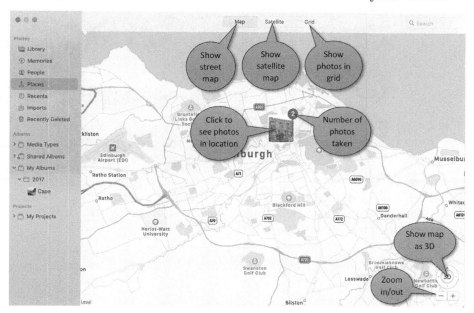

Here you'll see a map with markers on the map containing photos taken at that location. You can view on a street map or a satellite map, click the options on the toolbar at the top to change the map.

Double click on the marker to view all the photos taken in that location.

Double click photo to see larger or edit. Click the back arrow on the top left to go back.

You can also assign locations if your camera hasn't got a geo tagging feature. Select your images, right click on the selection and click 'get into'.

Click on 'assign a location' and type in the name of the city or location the photo was taken. Select the closest match from the drop down menu of suggested locations.

Now when you select 'locations' from the sidebar on the main screen, you'll see your photos appear across the world map according to the locations they were taken in.

Faces

The faces feature scans your photographs for recognisable faces and will show them as thumbnails on the people section. The Photos App will take a while to scan all your photos, so you'll need to wait for it to finish.

Once the Photos App has finished scanning all your photos, you'll notice a marker on each person's face when you open a photo. The Photos App will try to match the face with people in your contacts list. If there is no match you'll see an 'un named' marker.

Click on the marker and enter the person's name - select the closest match from the list that appears, if not press enter. This will train the Photos App to recognise these people in all your photos and any new ones that you take.

Do this for all your 'un named' photos.

Chapter 6: Using Multimedia

To see all your named photos, click 'people' on the side panel on the left hand side of your screen.

Double click on the thumbnail photo of the person to see all photos of them in your collection. Click 'show more' on the top right. Click a photo to see it full size.

To manually tag a face, open a photo from your photos library, then click the 'i' icon on the top right.

From the info panel, click 'add faces'.

You'll see a circular marker appear on top of the photo. Click and drag the small resize handle to resize the marker.

Click and drag it over the person's face.

The Photos App will attempt to identify this person in other photographs, so you don't need to tag multiple photos of the same person.

Memories

Memories are short slide show movies Photos App automatically creates, based on the time and place they were taken. You can add music and transitions between the photos to spice up your memories.

Create your Own Memory

To create your own memories, go to the 'Photos' tab and select all the photos you want to appear in your memory. You can select multiple photos by holding down the cmd key on your keyboard while selecting your photos.

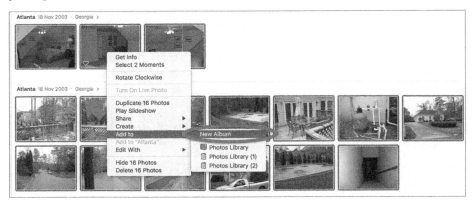

Right click on your selection, click 'add to' and select 'new album' from the slideout. Give the album a name, I'm going to call mine 'Thanks'. Your albums will show up under the albums section on the left hand side of the screen.

At the top of your album, click 'Show as Memory'.

Scroll right to the bottom of the page and click 'add to memories'.

Now when you go back to your memories section, you'll see your album has been added to your memories.

Right click on the image and select 'play slideshow'. Select a theme from the popup panel on the right hand side.

Click the 'music' tab, select a theme. If you want to include a track from your music library, click 'theme songs', change it to 'music'. Select the track you want from your library.

Once you have done that, click 'play slideshow'.

Smart Search

The smart search feature scans and analyses your photos to determine what objects the images contain. It will attempt to identify places, objects, animals, faces and will tag them accordingly.

This makes finding and grouping your photos so much easier. Type keywords into the search field on the top right of the screen.

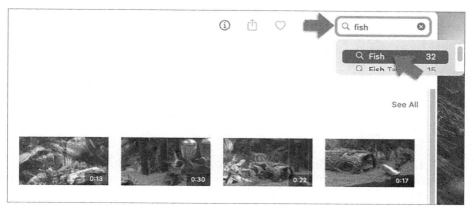

From the drop down, select a keyword. Type in another keyword or select another from the list to narrow your search.

You'll see a thumbnail list of all the photos that match the keywords you entered.

Sharing Photos

You can share your photos with your friends and family from within the Photos App. To do this, select the photos you want to share.

Click the share icon on the top right of the toolbar, then select the app you want to use to share the photos. I'm going to use email in this example. You can also use messages or airdrop.

Enter the names of the people you want to share the photos with into the 'to' field. Add a message at the top of the email if you want.

Select the image size to large to prevent the message from being too large.

Click the 'send' icon on the top left when you're done.

Shared Albums

A shared album creates a shared area where you can share photos with people. You can add photos to the shared album and you can allow others to add photos as well.

Select the photos and videos you want to share. Click the share icon on the top right of the toolbar, then click 'shared albums'.

Click 'new shared album'.

Type a name for the shared album (eg 'promo'), then type the email addresses of the people you want to share the album with. Click 'create'.

Now the people you shared the album with will get an invite in their email.

Chapter 6: Using Multimedia

You'll find your shared album under 'shared albums' on the sidebar. You can add photos and videos by dragging the photos to the shared folder on the sidebar.

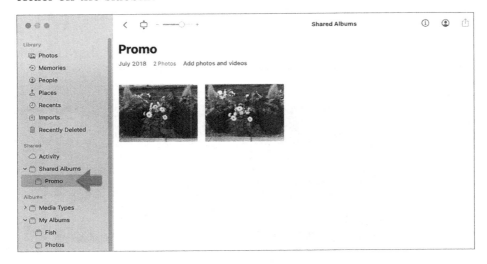

To edit the sharing options, click the shared folder on the sidebar, then click the 'people' icon on the top right of the toolbar.

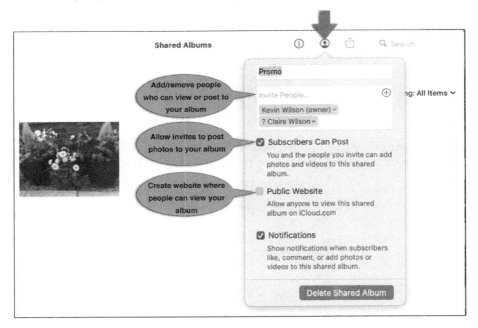

Click 'delete shared album' to delete the album. This only deletes the album not the actual images.

Printing Photos

To print photos, select the photos you want to print.

From the 'file' menu, then select 'print'.

From the print preview screen, select your printer on the top right, select paper size (eg A4), then select 'photo on photo paper'.

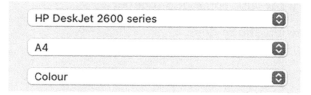

305

To get 4 photos on a page, select 'custom' from the layout options on the right hand side.

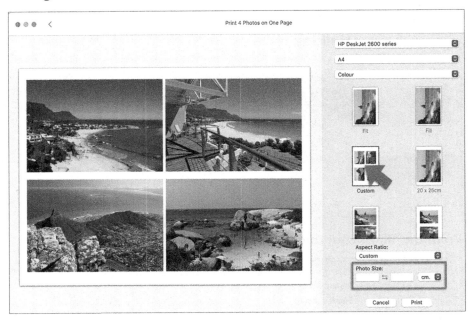

In the 'photo size' section, change the size of the photos to 9cm by 13cm. This will crop and fit four 9x13 photos onto a page.

You may need to adjust the sizes slightly to fit your page - adjust until all four photos appear on the page.

Load your printer with some photo paper.

Click 'print' when you're done.

Creating Slideshows

Select the photos you want, hold down the CMD key to select multiple photographs. Right click on the selection.

From the drop down menu select 'slideshow', go down to 'create' and select 'slideshow'.

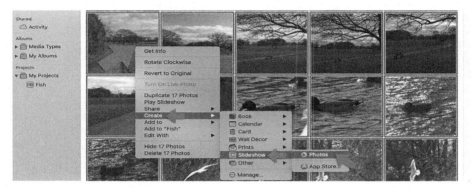

Give your slideshow a name

Double click the title text to edit the title.

Add some effects by clicking on the effects button on the right hand side, circled below far right.

In this example, I am going to apply a nice vintage photo look.

Click the music icon on the right hand side, indicated by the arrow, to add some music. You can add music from photos or you can use music from your music library.

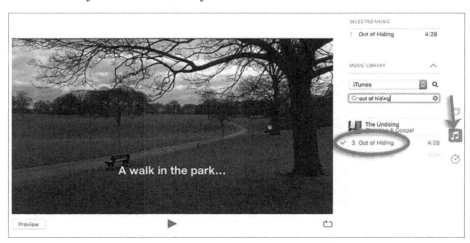

Hit the play button to run your slideshow. Now you won't have to bore your friends and family with your holiday/vacation pictures - you can create a more interesting slideshow.

Printing & Publishing Photos

Using the printing and publishing extensions you can create personalised projects such as photo books, calendars and greeting cards.

Installing the Apps

First you'll need to install the extensions, hover your mouse over 'my projects' on the left hand side of the screen. Select 'books', then click 'app store'.

Scroll down the 'print and publish your photos' screen until you see the apps. Install both 'mimeo photos' and 'motif'.

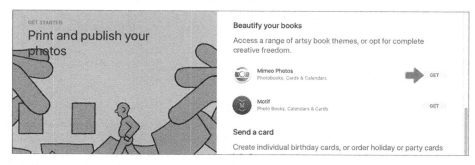

Click 'get' next to the app name. Click the green install button. Scroll down and install 'ifcolor photo products'.

Enter your Apple ID username and password if prompted.

Creating Photobooks

These make nice gifts at weddings, birthdays and special events. Select your photos from the main screen, hold down the CMD key to select multiple photographs. Right click on the selection, go down to 'create', select 'book' from the slideout, then click 'mimeo photos'.

Select a style then click 'create'.

Select 'autofill my photos' on the top right.

Select a theme.

310

Within the app, you can now start to create your book. You'll notice that the app has automatically added all your photos.

Double click 'add title here' and type in the title of your book.

Use the left and right arrows to move between pages.

Click 'photos' on the top right. From here you can drag and drop photos onto the pages to put them into the correct order.

Click the 'right' arrow to browse to the next page.

Chapter 6: Using Multimedia

To change the layout of the page, click the photo on the page where you want to change the layout, then select 'layout' from the right hand side panel.

Click 'page', select your page layout (eg 3 photos on page), then select how you want the photos arranged.

Now, select photos from the panel on the right. Drag and drop the photos you want into the placeholders.

To add a text caption, click the photo, then select 'text' from the panel on the right hand side. Click 'add empty text box'.

Drag the text box into position using the drag handle.

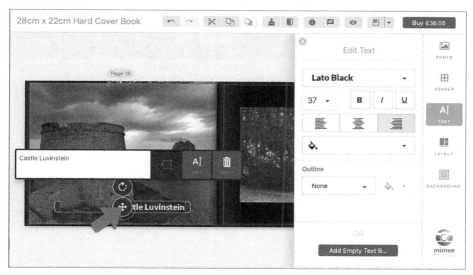

Change the font, size, colour using the 'edit text' panel on the right. Type your text into the textbox.

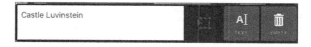

Click 'buy' on the top right when your book is complete.

Ordering Prints

Select the photographs you want to print, hold down the CMD key to select multiple photographs. It's best to order at least 10 to make the order worthwhile for the cost of printing and shipping.

Right click on your selection, go down to 'create'. From the slideout select 'prints', then click the 'ifcolor photo products' app.

Select your country, click 'next'.

Select 'create'.

If you want a bigger size, click on a photo, select a size.

Click the photos you want. Hold down the control key on your keyboard to select multiple photos. To select them all, press the command key on your keyboard, then press 'A'.

Click 'order' on the top right when you're done. Review your order, then click 'order' on the bottom right to confirm.

They'll post the prints to your address. You can frame and display them in your home if you wish.

Greeting Cards

You can create personalised greeting cards that are professionally printed. To create a card, select the image you want to use. Right click, select 'create' from the popup menu. Select 'card', then click 'mimeo photos'.

Select the type of card you want, eg 'folded landscape'.

Click 'create'.

Click 'autofill my photos', then select a theme.

Click the 'next' arrow on the bottom to jump to the interior of the card.

Here you can write your message. Double click in the grey placeholders and type your message in the text box.

Click 'buy' on the top right when you're done.

Continuity Camera

To use Continuity Camera, you will need to sign into all your Apple devices with the same Apple ID (eg Mac and iPhone). Also they will need to be connected to the same Wi-Fi network with Bluetooth enabled.

You can use continuity camera to quickly snap a photo with your iPhone or iPad and have it appear instantly on your Mac. This can be useful if you're writing a Pages document and need to insert a quick photo of something. You can also use continuity camera as a scanner, to scan in photos or documents and add hand drawn sketches.

Insert Photo from iPhone/iPad

In this demo, I'm going to insert a photo taken with an iPhone directly into a Pages document.

First open your Pages document. Right click where you want the photo to appear. From the popup menu, select 'take photo'.

You'll see a place-holder appear asking you to take the photo with your device

The camera app will open on your iPhone. Line up your shot, then tap the white circle to take the photo.

The photo will appear in the document.

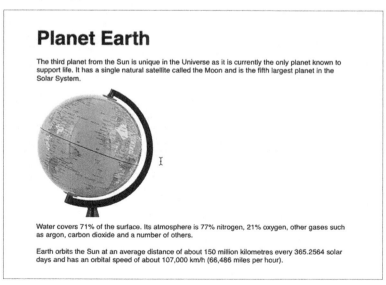

You can also scan documents using this feature, just choose 'scan documents' from the drop down menu instead of 'take photo'.

Add Sketch

For this demo, I'm going to insert a sketch from my iPad into a Pages document. To add a sketch, right click in the document where you want the sketch to appear, then select 'add sketch'.

Draw your sketch on your iPad or iPhone with your pencil or finger.

Tap 'done' on the top right of your iPad/iPhone screen. Your sketch will appear in the document on your Mac.

Scan a Document

To scan a document, right click in the desktop, go to 'import from ipad/iphone', then select 'scan document'.

Use your iPad/iPhone to scan the document. Line the document up in the yellow outline.

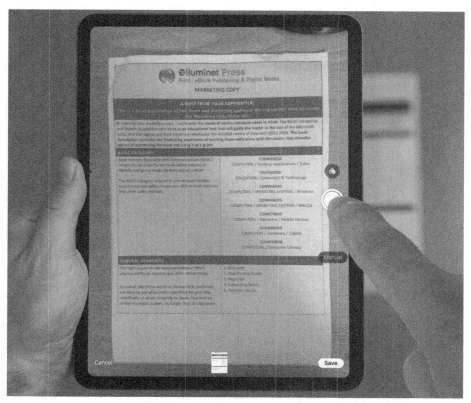

Tap 'keep scan', then scan the next page. When you've scanned all the pages, tap 'save' on the bottom right.

The scanned document will appear as a PDF on your Mac's desktop.

iMovie

iMovie is great for editing together your home movies. Perhaps you've just come back from your vacation/holiday, maybe a family member or friend has just got married, or maybe just collecting precious memories of your kids. You will find iMovie on launchpad or in finder.

If it's not installed, go to the app store and download it.

Importing Footage from your Camera

Connect the camera to your Mac with the USB cable. Turn your camera on and set it to 'PC Connect Mode' if required.

Now on your Mac, launch iMovie. Go to the file menu and select 'new movie'. Tap 'import media'.

Select your camera on the top left of the screen under the 'cameras' section. You'll see a thumbnail list of all the clips on your camera.

Select which video clips to import then click 'import selected'. To import all clips click 'import all'.

Importing Footage from your iPhone

To import video clips from your iPhone or iPad, you'll need to connect your device to your Mac using the USB cable.

Plug the cable into the bottom of your device, then plug the other end into a spare USB port on your Mac. You'll need to unlock your device with your Touch ID/Face ID, or passcode. When you do, you'll see a 'trust' prompt appear. Tap 'trust' to allow your Mac to access the media on your device.

Now on your Mac, launch iMovie. Go to the file menu and select 'new movie'.

Tap 'import media'.

Chapter 6: Using Multimedia

Select your device on the top left of the screen under the 'cameras' section. In this example, my iPhone is called 'ElluminetPress', so I'd select that one.

Here you can preview any clips and select the ones you want. Click 'import all' to import all your clips to your Mac.

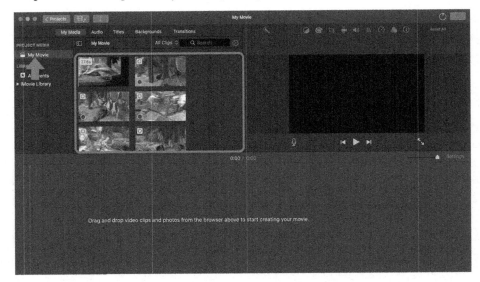

Once imported, you'll see all your clips in the project window.

Now you can start to drag and drop your clips into the timeline at the bottom of the screen to create your movie.

Adding Clips

To begin editing, click and drag a clip from your photo library or imported footage to the time line at the bottom of the screen.

Continue to add the clips you want to appear in your movie. You can also trim or cut out bits of the clips you don't want. For example, I want to add a part of the clip below. If you hover your mouse pointer over the clip, you'll see a yellow box appear with two handles either side - this is your trim box.

Click and drag the handle to mark the part of the clip you want. You'll see a preview of the clip play as you move your mouse - this is so you can see where in the clip you currently are.

Do the same for the end of the clip also.

Click and drag the clip you just trimmed to the time line. The clip will snap into place at the end.

Do the same with any other clips you want to add to your video.

Adding Titles

To add a title, select 'titles' from the icons along the top of the screen.

Click and drag the title you want to the position on the timeline where the title is to appear.

On the preview window on the right hand side, you'll see the title text markers. Type in your titles here.

Use the tool controls along the top to change font, size, colour, and so on.

Adding Music

To add a title, select 'audio' from the icons along the top of the screen.

From your music library, click and drag the track you want to the position on the timeline where the music is to start.

Transitions

You can also add transition effects between the clips. You can add a crossfade, wipe, or cut, along with various other transitions.

To add a transition, click the 'transition' icon along the top of the screen.

Drag the transition you want to one of the gaps between the clips on your timeline

To change the length of the transition, right click on the transition marker, and select 'precision editor' from the menu.

Now click on the yellow marker and drag it to the right to increase the length of the transition.

Click 'close precision editor', when you're done.

Animations

The only decent animation that is available is the map or globe. This is a nice feature to include in vacation/holiday videos, as you can set the location on the map to indicate where you've travelled to. You can also add backgrounds to titles.

To add an animation, click the 'backgrounds' icon along the top of the screen. Click and drag one of the map/globe animations to the position on the video the animation is to appear.

Double click on the animation in the timeline. You'll see a preview of the animation in the preview screen on the right hand side. Here you can customise it

Add your travel destinations in the route options at the top of the preview window.

Now when you play the animation, you'll see a map of your route.

Music App

Apple have split iTunes into three different apps: music app, podcasts app, and TV app. In this section we'll take a look at the Music App.

There are two ways you can buy your music. You can subscribe to Apple Music and stream any track you like from the music library for a monthly subscription fee. Or you can purchase and download the albums or tracks individually from the iTunes Store.

Subscribing to Apple Music

Let's take a look at Apple Music. With Apple Music you need a constant internet connection. At the time of writing, there are three subscription options for Apple Music.

- £4.99 a month gives you full access to the music library and is only available for University/College students.

- £9.99 a month gets you full access to the music library and many radio stations available. This is an individual account and allows only one account access to the iTunes Store.

- £14.99 a month gets you full access to the music library and radio stations and allows up to 6 people to sign in and listen to their music. This is ideal for families.

To sign up, open the Music App. From the list on the sidebar, select 'listen now'.

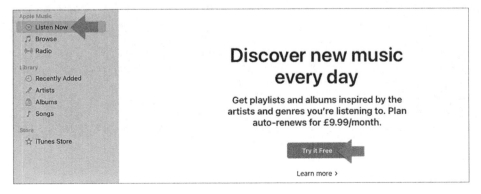

To get started, tap 'try for free', or 'start listening'.

Choose a membership programme, then tap 'start trial', or 'join apple music'.

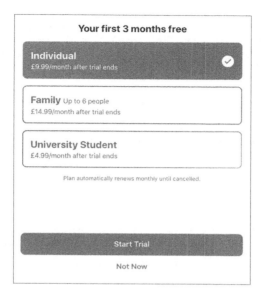

Enter your Apple ID username and password, or confirm with touch ID, if you have this enabled, by placing your finger on the home button.

The Main Screen

You can use the links under the 'apple music' section of the sidebar.

Here under 'listen now', you'll find curated playlists that have been compiled according to your listening habits. Click on the icons to view albums and tracks. Click 'browse' to browse through all the latest music releases. Click 'radio' to listen to various radio stations

Searching for Music

To search for an artist or band, type the name into the search field on the top left of the screen. Select the closest match from the list of suggestions.

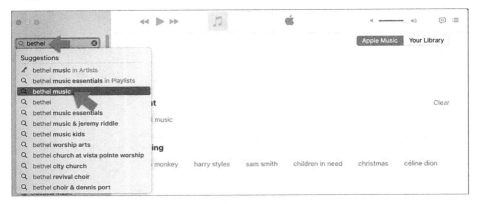

From here you can click on a song to listen to it, click and album to open it.

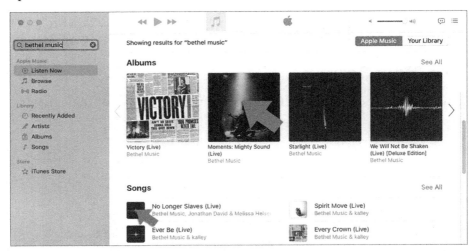

You'll see the track start to play at the top of the screen.

Add to Library

You can start to create a library of your favourite music, so it's easy to find. You can create a list of songs you want to listen to. To do this, tap the + sign next to the song you want to add to your library. If you want to add the whole album tap '+add'.

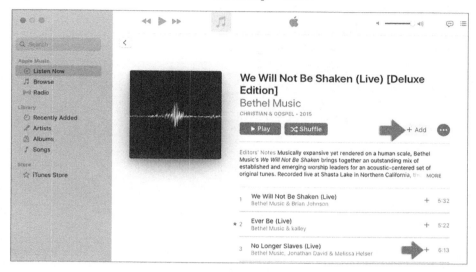

You can access your music library using the links under the 'library' section on the sidebar.

Select 'songs' to view the tracks you've added as a list, click albums to view as an album, click artists to view as artist.

Creating Playlists

You can create playlists to play all your favourite tracks from any album or artist.

To add a track to a playlist, click on the track in the list of songs, then from the popup menu, select 'add to a playlist.

Select the playlist you want to add the track to, if it exists. Or tap 'new playlist' to add the track to a new playlist.

You'll find the playlists under the 'playlist' section on the sidebar. Click the playlist to view the tracks. Click a track to start playing.

Importing CDs

Somewhat outdated technology nowadays, but if you still have audio CDs, you can import them. First you'll need an external CD drive. Plug the drive into a USB port on your Mac and insert a CD.

Open the music app on your Mac, your CD will appear under 'devices' on the left hand panel. Click on the CD to open. Click 'import CD' to begin.

Click 'ok' on the 'import settings' popup.

Import Settings

Import Using: MP3 Encoder

Setting: Higher Quality (192 kbps)

Details

96 kbps (mono) / 192 kbps (stereo), normal stereo.

☐ Use error correction when reading Audio CDs
Use this option if you experience problems with the audio quality from Audio CDs. This may reduce the speed of importing.

Note: These settings do not apply to songs downloaded from the iTunes Store.

Cancel   OK

Adding Tracks to your iPhone, or iPad Manually

Tracks you download from the iTunes Store or stream from Apple Music will automatically synchronise across your devices. If you want to add music you've imported from a CD or other source you can add the tracks to your device. To do this, plug your iPad or iPhone into your Mac using the USB cable.

On your Mac, open finder.

Select your iPad/iPhone from the left hand pane. Click 'trust' if prompted on your Mac and iPad.

336

Now, open the music app.

Select the tracks you want, then drag them to your iPad/iPhone under the devices section on the left hand side.

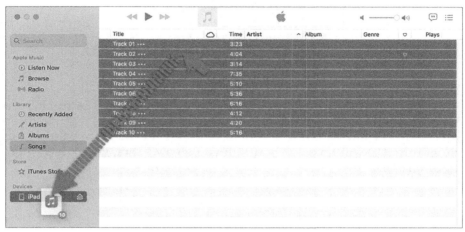

You'll be able to find the tracks on your iPad/iPhone.

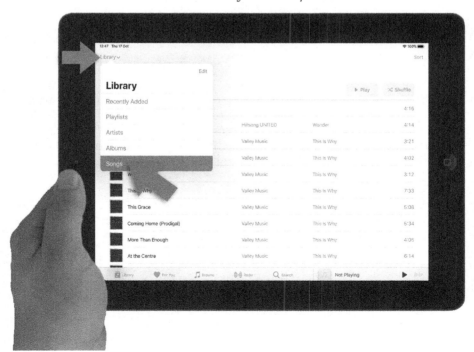

Burning CDs

CDs are somewhat outdated technology nowadays however, it is sometimes useful to burn tracks to a CD. Macs no longer include DVD/CD drives, so you'll need an external USB drive.

To do this, first you'll need to create a playlist with all the tracks you want on the CD. When adding music to your playlist, as a guide, keep an eye on the status bar at the bottom middle of the main window, an 80 minute CD will hold 1.2 hours. If you go over this, you'll need more than one CD.

'Use Sound Check' is useful when you have made a compilation of songs from different albums. It makes sure all the songs are at the same volume level, so you don't have to raise or lower the volume too much when you're listening to the CD in the car or on a CD player. Make sure 'Gap Between Songs' is set to none or automatic.

Insert a blank CD-R then click burn.

Podcasts App

A podcast is a series digital audio files and sometimes video files you can listen to. You can listen to all sorts of podcasts. To begin, click the podcasts icon on your dock or on launchpad.

Once the app starts, you can browse through the latest podcasts. Along the left hand side of the screen you'll see a side panel.

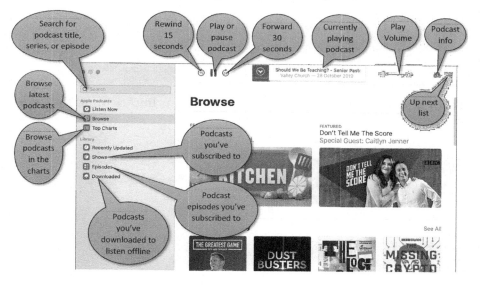

The best way to find your podcasts is to search for them. You can search for artist name, program name, or any area of interest. To search, click the search field on the top of the sidebar panel on the left hand side.

Type the podcast you're looking for in the search field at the top of the screen, the select the podcast you want from the results.

Chapter 6: Using Multimedia

Click 'subscribe' to get updates when new episodes are posted.

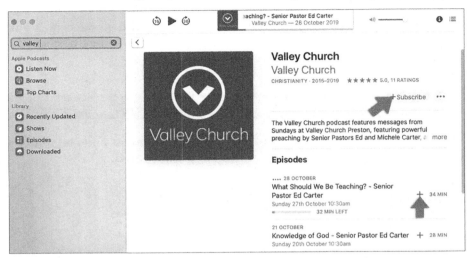

You'll find all your subscribed podcasts in your library or on the 'listen now' tab.

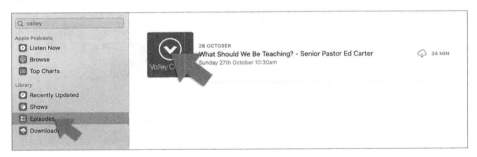

Click 'episodes' on the left hand side. You'll see a list of the episodes you've added. Click the podcast thumbnail to listen.

Hit the cloud icon next to the episode if you want to download the podcast to listen offline.

To delete a podcast, right click on the podcast and select 'remove'.

iTunes Store

If you've subscribed to Apple Music, you won't see the iTunes Store. To access the iTunes Store, open the Music App then click on 'iTunes Store' on the side panel on the left hand side of the screen.

Once the app has loaded you can browse through music, movies and tv shows - tap the category icons across the top of the screen. You can also type what you are looking for in the search field on the top right of the screen.

To search for your favourite tracks, artists and albums, click on the search field on the top left, then select 'iTunes Store' on the top right.

Type your search into the field at the top. Then select the closest match from the suggestions.

Along the top of the search results, you can view by song or album. Scroll up and down the list to see the songs and albums.

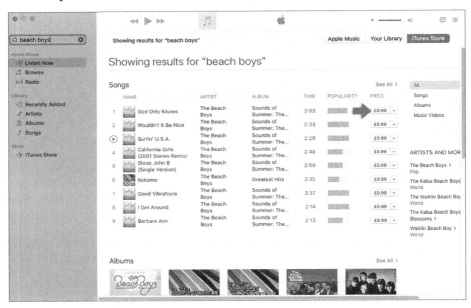

Click on the price tag to download the song. You'll need to enter your Apple ID email address and password to verify and confirm the purchase

Once the songs are downloaded you will find then in your recently added playlist under the 'library' section of the sidebar.

Apple TV App

Gearing up for Apple's new streaming service Apple TV+, the Apple TV App becomes your entertainment hub where you'll find all your purchased or rented films, music, and TV programmes. You'll find the app on your home screen.

Here, you'll be able to subscribe to Apple's streaming service and stream the latest TV Programmes and movies direct to your iPad.

Watch Now

When you first start the app, you'll land on the 'watch now' page.

Along the top of the screen you can select movies, tv shows, kids shows and your library of media you've purchased or rented. In the middle of the screen, you'll be able to scroll through current TV Shows and movie releases. Tap on the thumbnail icons to view details, or tap 'see more' on the top right to see more content.

Searching for Media

To search for a specific movie or tv show, type the name into the search field on the top right.

In the search results, click on the thumbnail cover to view the details.

On the film details screen you'll be able to read details about the film, reviews and ratings. Click 'rent' or 'buy'. Verify your purchase using your Apple ID username and password.

You'll find your downloaded films and TV programmes in the library section of the TV App.

Library

Select 'library' from icons along the top of the screen.

Select 'movies' to see movies you've rented or purchased, similarly select 'tv shows' if you've downloaded a tv show.

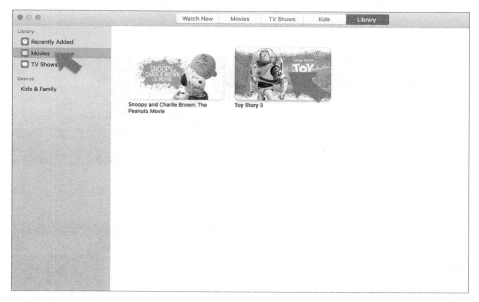

Tap on the movie or tv programme to begin playback.

Chapter 6: Using Multimedia

Apple TV+ Streaming

Apple TV+ is a video streaming service where you can subscribe and watch TV shows and movies.

Select 'watch now' from the icons along the top of the screen

Scroll to the Apple TV channels section and choose Apple TV+.

Select 'try it for free'.

Click 'confirm' on the dialog box, then enter your Apple ID email address and password when prompted.

Airplay

Airplay allows wireless streaming of audio and video data to an Apple TV or compatible receiver on your TV.

For this to work, both your iPad and Apple TV will need to be on the same WiFi network. This is usually the case in most homes.

To mirror your Mac, click the airplay icon on the bottom left of the play window during playback.

Select the tick box next to your Apple TV. Enter your Apple TV passcode if prompted.

347

If you don't know the Apple TV passcode, go on your Apple TV, then go to settings > Airplay, select 'Onscreen code'. You can turn off the code or set a new one.

Now you can watch your program on the big screen. Here below I have my Apple TV plugged into a digital projector. The Macbook on the right is streaming a movie to Apple TV.

Cancelling Subscriptions

First open the settings app.

From the settings app, select 'apple id' on the top right.

Select 'media & purchases', then next to 'subscriptions' click 'manage'.

Click 'edit' next to the subscription you want to cancel.

Click 'cancel subscription'.

Maintaining your Mac

In this section we'll take a look at some of the security aspects of Macs and how to go about putting it into practice.

We'll also look at some basic maintenance to keep your Mac running smoothly.

To help you better understand this section, take a look at the video resources. Open your web browser and navigate to the following site:

`videos.tips/sur-sys`

Firewalls

A firewall helps prevent unauthorised access to your Mac and works by monitoring incoming and outgoing network traffic according to a set of rules. A firewall won't protect you against malware and viruses, so adequate anti-virus software is still necessary but it is your first line of defence against a hacker trying to gain access to your computer or some malicious software trying to send data.

Enabling the Firewall

To set up your firewall, open the system preferences app and click 'Security & Privacy',

Click on the padlock and enter your admin password to unlock the settings.

Click on the firewall tab.

Click 'Turn On Firewall'.

Firewall Settings

To change the firewall settings, allow or block an app, follow the steps in the previous section, then click 'firewall options'.

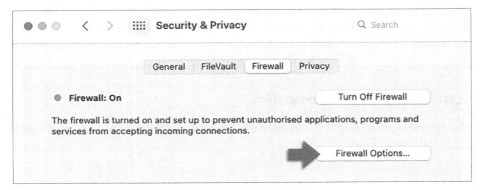

Here, you can block incoming connections, add or remove apps that are allowed, allow/deny signed apps to automatically connect, and enable stealth mode. Stealth mode hides your mac and prevents it from responding to probe requests from other machines on the internet.

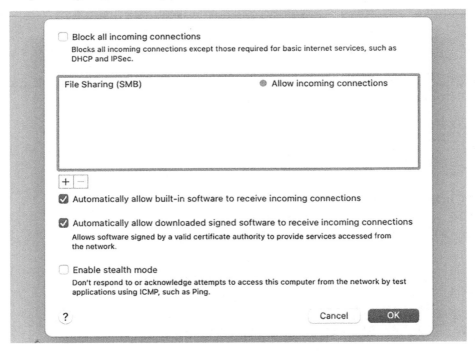

To allow an app through the firewall, click the + icon on the left, then select the app you want to allow from your Applications folder.

Do Apple Macs get Viruses?

Yes they do! The likelihood of a Mac getting a virus when compared to a Windows user is less, since there are more Windows users than Mac users. Although MacOS is more secure than many versions of Windows, it still has its own security vulnerabilities.

As Macs become more popular, more and more malware is being developed to target MacOS. Even though Macs are more secure, make sure you are protected, as you can still be a victim of trojan horses, phishing, ransomware and other online fraud. So don't fall victim to the 'macs don't get viruses' myth. Hackers and cyber thieves aren't after your computer, they're after your personal information so they can steal your identity, pin numbers and bank or credit card details. They'll try and trick you into handing this information over by pretending to be your bank, the IRS, or someone in authority. This is known as phishing. Learn to protect yourself, don't click on links in emails as these can be spoofed. Go directly to the site using the official URL and sign in.

A free simple anti virus for mac is Avast. There are a lot of different ones out there, but this one is free, small, fast and up to date so is a good place to start. It has a web shield to help protect you when you are browsing the web and warns you about websites that may have been compromised or reported as fake or fraudulent. It also has a email shield that scans incoming emails for worms and other threats.

You can download it here.

www.avast.com/mac

Once on their website, click the 'free download' link.

Go to the downloads folder in your finder and double click on the following file. `avast_security_online.dmg`

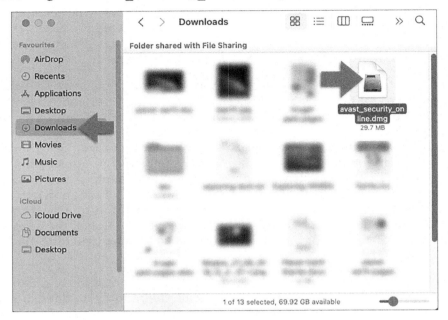

In the finder window that appears, double click on 'avast security' to install.

Follow the instructions on screen.

Downloading MacOS Big Sur

At the time of writing, you can download MacOS Big Sur free of charge from the App Store and upgrade your Mac automatically.

Go to the App Store and click the download link. If it isn't on the home page you can search for it. Type in 'macOS Big Sur'.

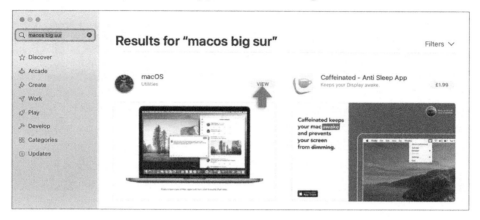

Click on 'view' next to 'macOS Big Sur'. On the details page click 'get' to start downloading Big Sur.

This download will take some time as it is about 5GB.

Installing MacOS Big Sur

Once you have downloaded the installer from the app store, you will be able to find it in finder/applications.

Click finder on the bottom left of your dock, then select 'Applications'.

Double click the installer circled above to start the installer.

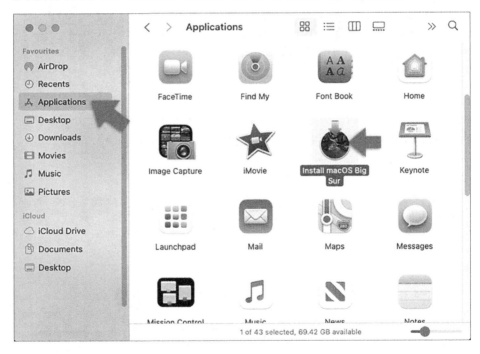

Follow the instructions on screen.

The installation will take a while. This is automated so you don't need to do anything.

Your mac may reboot a couple of times.

Once MacOS has installed, you'll need to run through the initial setup covered in 'starting your mac for the first time' section in chapter 2.

Create a Boot Drive

Creating a boot drive or recovery drive is always a good idea in case your mac crashes or your hard drive fails.

There is a very useful utility available on the internet, that will automatically create a boot drive on a USB memory stick or USB/ Flash drive.

Open safari web browser and go to the following website

diskmakerx.com/download/

Select the first download in the list.

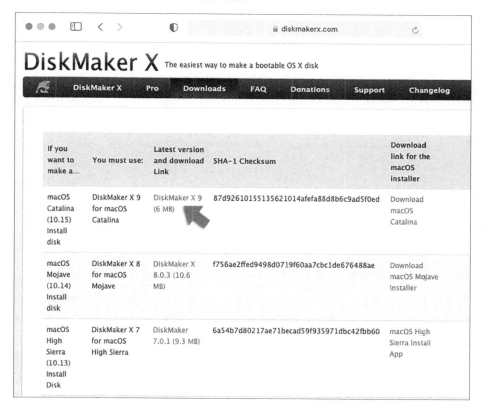

Once you have downloaded the utility, go to your downloads folder and run the following application...

DiskMaker_X_9.dmg

...and follow the on screen instructions.

Chapter 7: Maintaining your Mac

For this utility to work, you'll need to first download MacOS Big Sur from the app store. To download go to...

```
diskmakerx.com/download/
```

Select 'download macOS Big Sur' link.

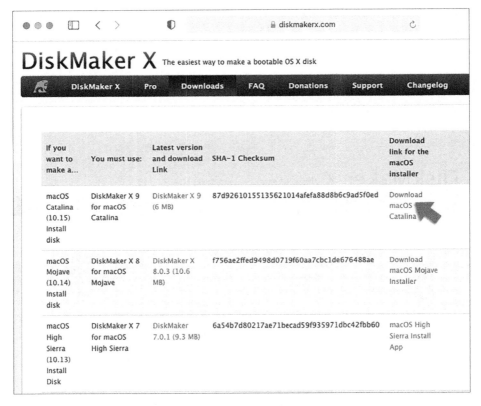

You'll need a flash drive that has at least 8GB available. Note that the diskmaker app will erase everything on the flash drive, so make sure it's one you don't use or have any important files on.

Open finder and go the applications folder on the left hand side. Double click 'DiskMaker X' icon to start the utility.

Select the version of Mac OS. Select the latest version available, either Catalina (10.15) or Big Sur (11.0).

Click 'select an OS X Installation App...'

Browse to your applications folder and select the Mac OS Big Sur Installer, indicated below. Then click 'choose'.

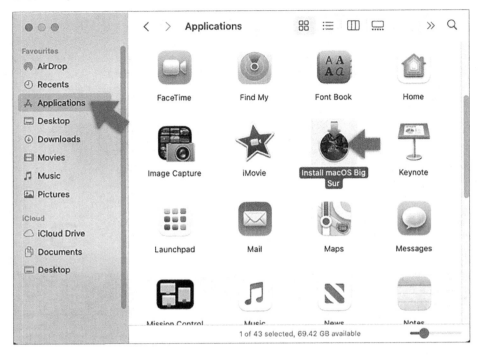

Click 'use 8GB USB thumb drive'.

Wait for the utility to create your installer.

DiskMaker X will prompt you with a notification once your drive is ready for use.

It will take a while to copy the required files.

Booting from a USB Drive

Now, to boot your Mac from the flash drive, insert the drive into a USB port and restart your mac.

When you hear the start up chime, hold down the Alt or Option key on your keyboard.

This will bring up the start up options menu.

Select your USB drive from the start up options.

Now you'll need to run through the set up procedure. Hit 'continue', and follow the on screen instructions.

Agree to the terms and conditions. Click 'agree'.

Select the disk you want to install Big Sur onto. This is usually your system disk and is already selected. Click 'install'.

Now, if you have a time machine backup, plug in your external drive, and select 'restore from time machine backup', otherwise click 'install macos' to install a brand new system from scratch. Click 'continue'.

If you selected 'restore from time machine backup', select your time machine backup disk from the list, then select the latest backup from the list.

Follow the instructions on the screen to finish installing MacOS Big Sur. Your Mac will restart itself a few times...

You'll need to run through 'starting your mac for the first time' in chapter 2.

Internet Restore

If you have replaced the hard disk on your Mac, or need to re-install MacOS, you can do this over the internet rather than creating a restore disk.

To do this, power up or reboot your Mac then quickly hold down **Command-Option-R** until you see the Spinning World Logo on the screen.

Once started, you'll land on the MacOS Utilities screen.

From here, you can install MacOS. Follow the instructions on screen. You'll need to run through 'starting your mac for the first time' in chapter 2.

Recovery Mode

If you need to reinstall MacOS or recover your Mac from a backup, you can boot into recovery mode.

To do this restart your Mac or turn it on. Hold down **Command** and **R**.

Here you can reinstall MacOS, restore from a time machine backup or repair a disk with the disk utility.

App Updates

To check if there are any updates for apps you have installed, open the app store and select the 'updates' option from the panel on the left hand side of the screen.

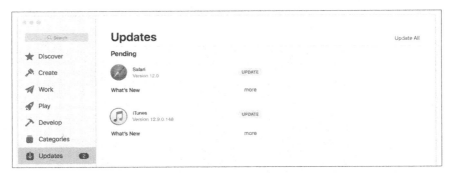

If any updates are available, they will be listed here.

To apply all the available updates, click 'update all' on the top right of the screen.

To apply updates to individual apps, click 'update' next to the update in the list.

System Updates

System updates such as security updates and macos updates, have been moved to its own section in the system preferences app

If there are any updates available, they will be listed here. Click 'update now' to apply the updates.

Select 'automatically keep my mac up to date' and MacOS will automatically apply the updates in the background. Select 'advanced' to select which updates to apply automatically.

Select them all, then click 'ok'. This will ensure your mac is always up to date and it will do this in the background without prompting you.

367

Mac Storage Management

The Storage Management window shows the current hard drive space and offers recommendations for optimising your storage.

Click the Apple menu on the top left, then select 'About This Mac'. On the window that pops up, select the 'storage' tab. Here, you can hover your mouse pointer over each of the coloured bars to see how much space it's taking up.

Click 'manage' on the top right of the window to manage your storage. Let's take a look at the recommendations.

Click 'store in icloud'. Here you can select between three options

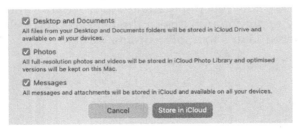

If you enable 'desktop and documents', when storage space runs low on your Mac, only the files you have recently opened are kept on your Mac, others are downloaded as you need them. Files stored only in iCloud are indicated with a small 'cloud' download icon. You can double click this to download the file to your Mac. If you enable 'photos', your Mac will store all original, full-resolution photos and videos in iCloud Photos. When storage space is needed, only the smaller, optimised versions are kept on your Mac. If you enable 'messages', this stores all messages and attachments in iCloud.

Lets take a look at the other options.

Optimise Storage, automatically remove watched films and TV programmes. When storage space is needed on your Mac, films or TV programmes purchased from the iTunes Store will be removed from your Mac.

If you turn on 'empty bin automatically' your Mac will permanently delete files older than 30 days.

Reduce Clutter helps you to identify large files and files you no longer use or need. Click 'review files'. Select from the tabs along the top of the window

Check in the 'downloads' tab and select a file you don't need anymore, then click 'delete'. Similarly in the 'large files' tab but use caution here and make sure that you no longer use or need these files. Videos and other large files are safe to delete as long as you don't use them anymore, just don't delete your iMovie, iTunes or Photo library if they show up.

Disk Utility

You can use the disk utility to partition, format or erase a hard disk. You can also use the disk utility to scan a disk for errors and effect repairs. This utility should be used with caution as misuse can cause data loss.

To start the disk utility, open launch pad and select 'other'.

Click 'disk utility' to start the app.

Lets take a look at the app.

Select a disk from the panel on the left hand side. From here, you can scan your disks for errors using the 'first aid' icon on the toolbar. You can also partition and format new disks as well as external disks and flash drives.

Checking Drives

To check a drive for errors, select the drive from the side panel, then click the 'first aid' icon on the toolbar.

Formatting Drives

If you have a new drive, external drive, or flash drive, you'll need to format it first.

To format a drive, select the drive from the side panel, then click the 'erase' icon on the toolbar.

Make sure you select the correct drive as formatting will erase any data on the disk.

Give the drive a meaningful name. Click the drop down menu next to 'format'.

Select a disk format. If you are going to use your drive only on a Mac, choose MacOS Extended (journaled) or APFS. If you are formatting an external drive and intend on using it on different machines such as Windows, Mac, or Linux, use ExFAT.

Click 'security options' on the bottom left.

The security options allow you to select how secure the erase operation is. Drag the slider to the right to select the options.

Option 1 does not securely erase the files on the disk. A disk recovery application may be able to recover the files. Useful for every day data.

Option 2 writes a pass of random data, and then a single pass of zeros over the entire disk. It erases the information used to access your files and writes over the data two times. Useful for every day data.

Option 3 writes 2 passes of random data followed by a single pass of known data over the entire disk. It erases the information used to access your files and writes over the data 3 times. Useful if the drive contains sensitive information.

Option 4 erases the information used to access your files and writes over the data 7 times. Useful if the drive contains sensitive information.

Click 'erase' when you're done. The disk utility will format your drive.

Partitioning Drives

A partition is just a fancy word for a storage space on a disk drive. Drive partitioning allows users to divide a physical disk drive into multiple storage spaces.

You can partition a drive using the disk utility. To do this, select the drive you want to partition in the sidebar, then click the partition icon.

Select 'partition' from the dialog box if prompted.

You'll see the current partition information for the drive you selected. .

To resize the current partition, hold down the command key on your keyboard, click and drag the resize handle at the top of the pie chart on the left hand side. Note you can't resize FAT or ExFAT formats.

To create a new partition, click the '+' icon on the bottom left.

The pie chart on the left will divide into two halves. In the name field on the right enter a name for the partition. Set the disk format (eg MacOS Extended (journaled), APFS or ExFAT).

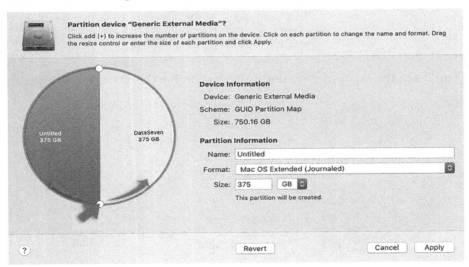

Click 'apply'.

FileVault

FileVault allows you to encrypt the data on your Mac with 256-bit encryption to help prevent unauthorized access to your data. Any subsequent changes to your data will be automatically encrypted. If you have an Mac with a T2 chip, data on your drive is already encrypted automatically. You'll only be able to access the data with your login password or encryption key.

To set up filevault, open the system preferences app and click 'Security & Privacy'.

Click the 'filevault' tab, then click the lock on the bottom left. Enter your mac username and password (an admin mac username and password is required).

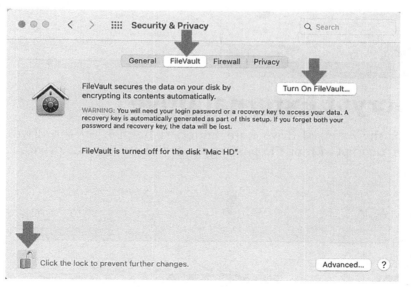

Click 'Turn On FileVault'.

Now select 'allow my iCloud account to unlock my disk', then click 'continue'. This is the safest way. If you lose or forget your password, you can still reset your password and recover your data. If you lose a recovery key your data is lost.

MacOS will begin to encrypt your disk. This can take a while.

Encrypt External Drive

This will work on any external drive formatted using 'APFS' or 'MacOS Extended (journalled)' format with a 'GUID partition map' scheme.

Plug in the drive, open finder, right click on the drive, then select 'encrypt'.

Decrypt External Drive

Select the external drive from finder, right-click on the drive, then select 'decrypt'. Enter the password used to encrypt the drive.

Reset SMC

The SMC or System Management Controller, is responsible for controlling the power button, battery, temperature control of internal components, keyboard backlight, video sources, fan speed, and various status indicators.

If your Mac doesn't respond when you press the power button even if it's plugged in, shuts down unexpectedly or is generally running slowly, you can try reset the SMC.

New Macbooks (2018+)

For MacBook Pro and MacBook Air models released in 2018 or later with T2 chip

First shut down your Mac.

On your keyboard hold down:

Left Control, Left Option, Right Shift, and the Power Button

Hold these down for 7 seconds.

Release all the keys, then press the power button again to start your Mac as normal.

Older Macbooks

For MacBook Pro models released mid-2009 to 2017 and MacBook Air models released in 2017 or earlier

First shut down your Mac.

On your keyboard hold down:

Left Shift, Left Control, Left Option and the Power Button

Hold these at the same time for 10 seconds.

Release all the keys, then press the power button again to start your Mac as normal.

iMac, Mac Pro and Mac Mini

First shut down your Mac.

Disconnect the power cable.

Press and hold the power button for 5 seconds.

Reattach the power cables and start Mac as usual.

Reset NVRAM

NVRAM or Non-volatile Random Access Memory, is a small memory chip on your Mac that is used to store time zone, sound volume, startup-disk, and other settings.

If you experience issues related to these settings or others, resetting NVRAM might help. For example, if your Mac starts up from a disk drive other than the one selected in Startup Disk preferences, or a question mark icon briefly appears before your Mac starts up, you might need to reset NVRAM.

First, shut down your Mac.

Press the power button to start your Mac, then quickly hold down:

Option, Command, P, and R

Hold these keys for about 20 seconds, during which your Mac might appear to restart. You'll hear two start up chimes.

Release the keys after you hear the second chime or see the Apple logo.

Video Resources

To help you understand the procedures and concepts explored in this book, we have developed some video resources and app demos for you to use, as you work through the book.

To find the resources, open your web browser and navigate to the following website

`videos.tips/mac-os-sur`

At certain points in the book you'll find a website link that will allow you to navigate to the relevant video demo.

Type the website url into the address bar at the top of your browser.

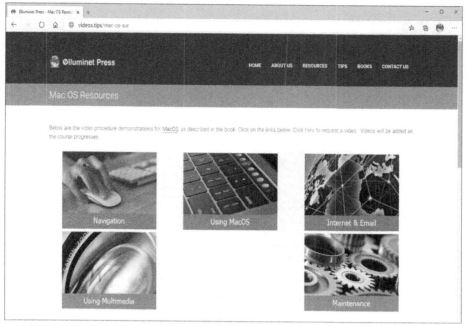

You'll see different categories. Click on these to access the videos.

When you open the link to the video resources, you'll see a thumbnail list at the bottom.

Click on the thumbnail for the particular video you want to watch. Most videos are between 40 and 90 seconds outlining the procedure, others are a bit longer.

Appendix A: Video Resources

When the video is playing, hover your mouse over the video and you'll see some controls...

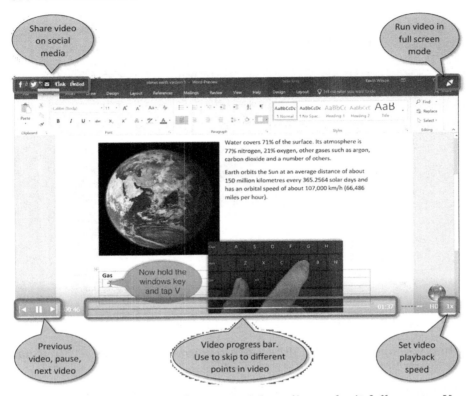

Here, you can share the video on social media, make it full screen. You can also play/pause the video, jump to a particular part of the video using the progress bar and set the playback speed.

You'll also find cheat sheets

Here, you'll find short-cuts, updates and tips.

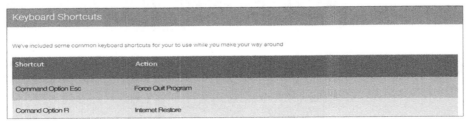

You'll also find a tips section. Here, we'll keep you up to date with the latest tips and tricks to help you get the most out of windows 10.

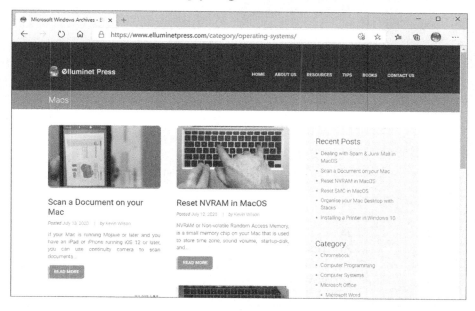

Finally, you'll find a glossary of computing terms.

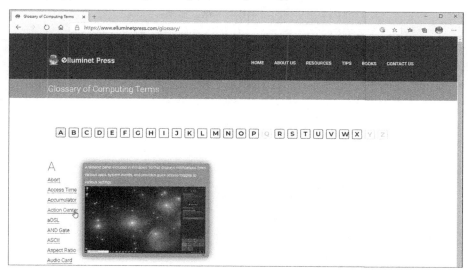

You can find the index here:

www.elluminetpress.com/glossary

This is integrated into the resources section.

Index

A

Address Book 267
Air Drop 279
Airplay 347
APFS 372
Apple Books 194
Apple ID 32
Apple ID Password 60
Apple Music 330
   Subscribing 330
Apple Pay 61, 153
Apple TV+ 346
Apple TV App 343
   Searching for Media 344
   Watch Now 343
   Your Library 345
Application Menu 96
App Store 182
App Updates 366
Audio 76
Auto Unlock 154

B

Backup
   Restoring Items 89
   Setting Up Backups 85
Backup Files 85
Backups 85
Bluetooth 78

Blu-Ray 120
Blu-rays 208
Books 194
Boot Drive 357
   Create a Boot Drive 357
Booting from a USB Drive 361

C

Calendar 200
   Add an Event from Email 202
   Adding an Event 200
   Create a Calendar 201
   Creating Public Calendars 204
   Export Calendar 201
   Import Calendar 202
   Public Calendar 203
   Sharing Calendars 204
Cancelling Subscriptions 349
CDs 120
Change Passwords 59
Changing Desktop Background 71
Clipboard 148
Close a Window 134
Colour Profiles 75
Command Key 156
Compress Files 118
Contacts 267
   Add a Contact from Scratch 268
   Add Email Contact from Apple Mail 270
   Creating Groups 269
Continuity Camera 318
   Add Sketch 320
   Insert Photo from iPhone/iPad 318
   Scan Document 321
Control Centre 140
   Add Controls to Control Centre 141
   Add Control to Menu Bar 140
   Open Control Centre 140
Control Key 157

D

Dark Mode 66
Decrypt External Drive 376
Desktop 95
Desktop Wallpaper 72

Index

Dictation 151
Disk Utility 370
   Checking Drives 371
   First Aid 371
   Formatting Drives 371
   Partitioning Drives 373
     Create New 374
     Resize 374
Display Arrangement 74
Display Calibration 75
Display Colour Profiles 75
Display Resolution 73
Display Rotation 73
Dock 97
   Add an App 98
   Change Size 97
   Recently Used Apps 97
   Re-Order Apps 99
   Stacks 98
Downloading MacOS 355
DVDs 120, 208
Dynamic Desktop 71
   Change Background 71

E

Email
   Attachments 261
   Blind Carbon Copies 257
   Carbon Copies 260
   Emojis 261
   Format Email 260
   Forward 259
   Markup 264
   New Email 260
   Replying 258
   Spam 266
   Threads 256
Email Accounts 52
Encrypt External Drive 376
Ethernet 38, 39
ExFAT 372
External Drives 119

F

Facetime 271
   Answering Calls 273

Calling Someone New 272
Group Facetime 274
Placing Video Calls 271
Filename Extensions 126
FileVault 375
Finder 104
Connect to a Server 124
Desktop Icons 125
Filename Extensions 126
Markup 108
Preferences 125
Quick Preview Files 118
Shared Folders 124
Sidebar Shortcuts 126
Smart Folders 115
Tags 112
Change colour 112
Create new tag 113
Rename 113
Tagging Files 114
View 105
Find My 81
Locating 82
Setup 81
Sharing Locations 83
Taking Action 82
Firewalls 351
Enabling the Firewall 351
Settings 352
Allow or Block Apps 352
Stealth Mode 352
Fonts 79
Download 80
Install 79
Formatting Drives 371
Frozen Apps 181
Function Key 157

G
Gestures 160
Four Finger Open 162
One Finger Point and Tap 160
Right Click 160
Two Finger Rotate 161
Two Finger Scroll 161

Index

Two Finger Swipe 162
Gmail 52

H
Handoff 142
  Setup 142
  Using 143

I
iBooks 194
iCal 200
iCloud 33
  Buy Storage 36
  Delete Data 36
  iCloud Drive Setup 34
  iCloud Sync 35
  Sign in/out 33
  Storage Management 36
iCloud Drive 127
  File Sharing 129
  iCloud Drive Setup 34
  Using iCloud Drive 127
Image Capture 205
iMessage 275
iMovie 322
  Adding Clips 325
  Adding Music 327
  Adding Titles 326
  Animations 329
  Importing Footage from your Camera 322
  Importing Footage from your iPhone 323
  Transitions 328
Initial Setup 25
Installing MacOS 356
Internet 37
iTunes Store 341

K
Keyboard 156
Keyboard Shortcuts 158
Keychain 176
Keynote App 225
  Adding a New Slide 227
  Adding Media 227
  Adding Styles to Textboxes 232
  Animations 228

Editing a Slide 226
Formatting Text Boxes 230
Formatting Text Inside Textboxes 231
Getting Started 225
Saving 234
Transitions 230

L

Launching Apps 100, 179
Launchpad 100
    App Groups 100
    Organize Apps 100
    Search 101
Light Mode 66
Login Options 57
Low disk space 368
LTE 42

M

MacOS Extended (journaled) 372
Mac Password 59
Mail 255
    Attachment 261
    Blind Carbon Copies 257
    Carbon Copies 260
    Emoji 261
    Formatting your Message 260
    Forward 259
    Junk Mail 266
    Mail Drop 262
    Markup 264
    Photo from Photos App 262
    Replying 258
    Threads 256
    Writing an Email 260
Maps 185
    3D 193
    Driving Directions 191
    Drop a Pin 187
    Favourites 187
    Finding Places 185
    GPS 193
    Guides 188
    Look Around 192
    Look Inside 193
    Public Transport Routes 190

Index

    Share a Location 186
    Walking Directions 192
Markup 108
Maximise a Window 134
Menu Bar 96
    Application Menu 96
    Status Menu 96
Message App 275
    Emojis 275
    Memojis 277
    Message Effects 278
    New Message 275
    Send Files 276
    Sending Files 276
    Sending New Messages 275
Microsoft Account 52
Migration Assistant 90, 93
Minimise a Window 134
Mission Control 102
Models 18
    iMac 19
    iMac Pro 19
    Macbook Air 18
    Macbook Pro 18
    Mac Mini 19
    Mac Pro 19
Mouse 69, 163
    Find your Mouse Pointer 165
    Left Click 163
    Right Click 163
    Scrolling 164
    Swipe 164
Moving a Window 132
Music App 330
    Adding Tracks to your iPhone, or iPad 336
    Add to Library 333
    Burning CDs 338
    Creating Playlists 334
    Importing CDs 335
    Searching for Music 332
    The Main Screen 331

N
Network 121
News App 214
Night Shift 75

Notes 198
   Add Check Box 199
   Add Table 199
   Collaborate 199
   Photos 199
Notification Centre 136
   Alerts 137
   Badges 137
   Banners 137
   Settings 138
   Widgets 139
Numbers App 235
   Building a Spreadsheet 237
   Changing Data Types 238
   Entering Data 237
   Formulas 238
   Functions 239
   Saving 239
NVRAM 379

O

Optimise Storage 368
Option Key 157

P

Pages App 218
   Adding a Picture 221
   Collaboration 224
   Formatting Text 220
   Getting Started 218
   Instant Alpha 222
   Saving 223
Partitioning Drives 373
Password Manager 176
Passwords 59
Peripherals 45
Personal Hotspot 41
Phishing 353
Phone 281
Photobooth 206
Photos App 283
   Adding Filters 289
   Adjusting Photos 286
      Brightness 286
      Color 288
      Contrast 287

Index

Exposure 287
Shadows 287
White Balance 288
Faces 295
Manually Tag a Face 296
Naming People in Photos 295
View photos of a person 296
Folders and Albums 290
Adding Photos 292
Creating 290
Importing your Photos 284
Memories 298
Creating 298
Places 293
Assign a Location to Photo 294
Map 293
Viewing photos by place 293
Printing Photos 305
Publishing Photos 309
Greeting Cards 316
Installing the Apps 309
Ordering Prints 314
Photobooks 310
Search 301
Shared Albums 303
Sharing Photos 302
Slideshows 307
Podcasts App 339
Add to Library 340
Removing Podcasts 340
Search for Podcasts 339
Subscribing 340
Power Down 24
Power Up 23
Preferences 47
Printers 49

R

Ransomware 353
Recovery Mode 366
Re-Install MacOS 365
Resizing a Window 133
Restore 365
Right Click 163

S

Safari 241
    Autofill Forms 254
    Bookmarking Pages 244
    Browsing Tabs 243
    Close Tab 243
    Customise your Homepage 242
    Downloads 248
    Extensions 249
    Launching Safari 241
    Open a link in a new tab 243
    Organising Bookmarks 247
    Passwords 251
        Generate Automatic Strong Passwords 253
        Managing Passwords 252
    Privacy 250
    Reading List 248
    Revisiting Bookmarked Sites 246
    Searching the Web 243
    Show all Browsing Tabs 244
    Switch to Tab 243
Scan Document 321
Screen Arrangement 74
Screen Calibration 75
Screen Colour Profiles 75
Screen Recording 171
Screen Resolution 73
Screen Rotate 73
Screensavers 70
Screenshots 170
Search 135
Second Display 74
Second Screen 74
Sharing Files on a Network 121
SideCar 144
    Send Apps to your iPad Screen 146
    Setup 144
    Setup Displays 147
    Using with iPad 145
Sign a Document 174
Siri 149
SMC 377
Sound 76
Spaces 102
Spam 266

Index

Split Screen Mode 172
Spotlight 135
SSID 51
Stacks 99
Starting your Mac for the First Time 25
Startup Keys 159
Status Menu 96
Storage Management 368
System Preferences 47
System Updates 367

T
Terminal 216
Tethering 41
Time Machine Backup
     Restoring Items 89
     Setting Up Backups 85
Touch Bar 166
     Application Strip 167
     Control Strip 167
     Customise 169
     Layout 166
Touch ID 64
Trackpad 67, 160
     Four Finger Open Launchpad 162
     One Finger Point and Tap 160
     Two Finger Rotate 161
     Two Finger Scroll 161
     Two Finger Swipe 162
Transfer Files from an old Mac 93
Transfer Files from a Windows PC 90
TV+ 346

U
Universal Clipboard 148
Unresponsive Apps 181
Updates 366
USB-C ports 45
USB Modems 42
Users 55

V
Virtual Desktops 102
Viruses 353
Voice Control 150
Voice Memos 210